JAMIE ADLER

IN THE
GAME

*24 Short Stories About The
Extraordinary Game Of Basketball*

Copyright © 2023 by Jamie Adler

All rights reserved. No part of this publication may be reproduced or transmitted in any form or by any means, electronic or mechanical, including photocopying, recording, scanning or otherwise, or through any information browsing, storage or retrieval system, without permission in writing from the publisher.

978-1-915217-34-9 – Basketball (paperback)

Scan the QR code below for a FREE copy of 'Hoops Harmony: A basketball short story playlist'

Table of Contents

Prologue 7

Introduction 9

Chapter 1: The Birth of Basketball 16

Chapter 2: When the Court Was a Cage 20

Chapter 3: Seven Seconds or Less: How the Suns Introduced the Modern Style 24

Chapter 4: The Legacy of Bill Russell 29

Chapter 5: The First Hoopers 33

Chapter 6: The Iconic NBA Logo 38

Chapter 7: Playing Above the Rim: The Connection Between Height and Basketball 43

Chapter 8: A Game for Everyone: The Rise of Women's Basketball 50

Chapter 9: The Unstoppable Wilt 57

Chapter 10: Dreaming of Gold: At the Olympics 62

Chapter 11: The Answer: Allen Iverson 70

Chapter 12: The Secret Game 76

Chapter 13: Bird, Magic, and the '80s Revival 80

Chapter 14: Jersey Story 84

Chapter 15: The GOAT: Michael Jordan 89

Chapter 16: Remembering Kobe 100

Chapter 17 The Rise of Yao Ming and the Asian Influence 113

Chapter 18: When the Game Gets Real: Medical Emergencies and Tragedies on the Court 117

Chapter 19: The Art of Slam Dunks 123

Chapter 20: All About Kareem 130

Chapter 21: The Show Goes On: Harlem Globetrotters 135

Chapter 22: How Basketball Changes Lives 140

Chapter 23: Impact of Basketball on Hip-hop Culture............................... 148

Chapter 24: From Lucky Socks to Superstitions: Inside the Quirky World of Basketball Rituals 153

Conclusion 159

References 164

Prologue

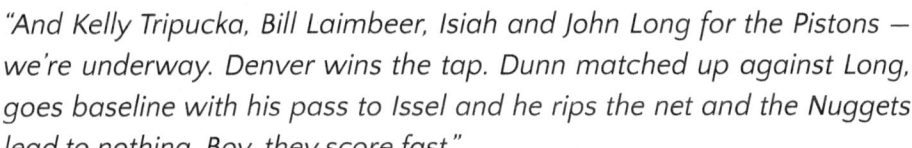

"And Kelly Tripucka, Bill Laimbeer, Isiah and John Long for the Pistons — we're underway. Denver wins the tap. Dunn matched up against Long, goes baseline with his pass to Issel and he rips the net and the Nuggets lead to nothing. Boy, they score fast."

"Fast and a lot of them you've got to be ready to play defense. When you play against these guys, you can't relax at all."

"Pistons come down and set up the cross order from Isiah to John Long and John ties it at two. Rob Williams (is) trying to push it up. Issel has it on top, a pump faker to drive and two more on Laimbeer!"

"The old man's supposed to have his back hurt but evidently, he's got a corset or something on, because it doesn't look like it's bothering him at all."

"Pistons strive for the tie, they go mid-post to Laimbeer, he guns over Issel, gets it and we are tied at four. What a start!"

"Well nobody's gonna miss. Rob Williams trying to snake down the lane against the Pistons, draws contact."

"I think that's going to be on Levingston, George."

"It is."

"That's the kind of situation that Cliff has found himself in a lot where you know he's not playing the minutes that we need him to play because he's

getting in foul trouble and those are the kind of foul [audio missing]"

"...for Denver. Just underway, a minute's been played. Kelly Tripucka sends it low left, Laimbeer and he gets it down tied at six."

"Nobody's missed yet!"

"Uh-uh. Dan Issel will try again and he'll score again from the wing for the Nuggets! It is 8-6 and we have played just over a minute."

"And it's got to get you pumped up, George, I'll tell you, when I played, I used to love offense too."

"Laimbeer finally with a miss, hollers for a foul call, doesn't get it, Nuggets rip the rebound down, Rob Williams nearly drops it. Vandeweghe gets it, goes in the lane, gets some Tripucka contact and a foul on Kelly. Misses the shot."

"Tough situation right there simply because Kiki really forced that shot because he had three Detroit players around him and he was of the frame of mind where he followed through and that's where Kelly hit him on the arm on the follow-through."

"Vandeweghe hits the first free throw and Denver's suddenly up three. He gets the next and it's Denver by 4, 10-6. Ten and a half to play in the first."

This is the first few minutes of the Detroit Pistons versus Denver Nuggets game in December 1983. It wasn't an ordinary game – it was the highest-scoring game in NBA history. Although it was just a regular-season affair, the pace resembled that of an NBA All-Star game. It was played at a frenetic pace with both teams lighting up the scoreboard at will. Once the final buzzer sounded, the game became firmly entrenched in the NBA record books.

"That game lasted so long, we were wondering if we could find a place to eat after the game. We were wondering, 'Is there an all-night diner in Denver?'" – Detroit Pistons forward Kelly Tripucka on his team's 186-184 triple-overtime win over the Denver Nuggets on December 13th, 1983.

Introduction

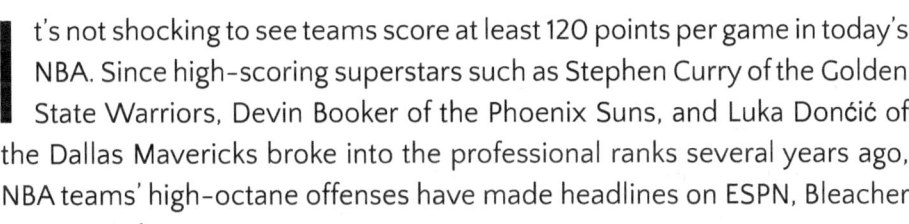

It's not shocking to see teams score at least 120 points per game in today's NBA. Since high-scoring superstars such as Stephen Curry of the Golden State Warriors, Devin Booker of the Phoenix Suns, and Luka Dončić of the Dallas Mavericks broke into the professional ranks several years ago, NBA teams' high-octane offenses have made headlines on ESPN, Bleacher Report, and NBA.com.

As much as we love watching our favorite players shoot the lights out, it's rare for teams to combine for almost 400 points in a single game. Unbelievably, that's exactly what the Detroit Pistons and Denver Nuggets did at McNichols Sports Arena in Denver, CO, on December 13, 1983.

That game featured the Nuggets' Kiki Vandeweghe, Alex English, Danny Schayes, Dan Issel, and Bill Hanzlik. The Pistons had a young Isiah Thomas, John Long, Kelly Tripucka, Cliff Levingston, Bill Laimbeer, Vinnie Johnson, and Lionel Hollins. Nobody would have predicted the two teams would blow up the stat sheet on that cold winter evening in the Mile-High City.

Final score: Pistons 186, Nuggets 184, in triple-overtime.

According to ESPN, the game lasted three hours and eleven minutes. A typical forty-eight-minute NBA game lasts two hours and thirty minutes in real time. Think about that for a minute – the Pistons and Nuggets showdown lasted as long as a typical National Football League (NFL) game.

Now, it's not unusual to see a score of 186-184 during an NBA All-Star Game when the game's best players slack off a bit and play lackadaisical defense because team standings and playoff hopes are not at stake. I consider some of the more recent NBA All-Star Games unwatchable because they're like a circus, where the stars just have fun and light up the scoreboard at will.

However, bear in mind the Nuggets-Pistons game was played just six weeks into a grueling eighty-two-game season. When you look at the game's final box score, it's obvious the players were just starting their six- or seven-month grind into May or June if they made the playoffs.

The 6'1" Thomas, one of the most intense short players in league history, torched Denver for forty-seven points. Long and Tripucka weren't far behind with forty-one and thirty-five points for the Pistons, respectively.

For their part, Vandeweghe (fifty-one points) and English (forty-seven points) combined for nearly 100 points for Denver. Unfortunately, their efforts proved futile in the end.

Each NBA team has an eighty-two-game regular-season schedule. When you multiply that number by the current number of NBA teams (thirty), the answer is 2,460 – the total number of regular-season NBA games in a year. It takes true grit and greatness to exceed at that level – no wonder guys like Thomas and English were NBA All-Stars year in and year out back in the day.

Those guys were a cut above the rest. They personified the demands and rigors of NBA basketball because of their incredible physical and mental attributes. While I was no Detroit Pistons fan growing up in the 1980s, I marveled at Thomas's twenty-five-point quarter against Magic Johnson's Los Angeles Lakers in the 1988 NBA Finals. He pulled that off despite a nagging ankle injury. Thomas, in a nutshell, was the epitome of perseverance despite insurmountable odds.

Players like Isiah Thomas, "Pistol" Pete Maravich, Dominique Wilkins, Jason "White Chocolate" Williams, Michael Jordan, and Clyde Drexler not only proved they stood head and shoulders above the competition, but their diverse backgrounds reflected the game of basketball on a wider scale – it welcomes the best players in, regardless of their various upbringings.

That's what makes basketball such a global game: it brings unique perspectives and playing styles to the hardwood. During my formative years, I saw guys like Sudan's Manute Bol, Romania's Gheorge Muersan, Canada's Steve Nash, France's Tony Parker, China's Yao Ming, and Lithuania's Šar·nas Mar·iulionis strut their stuff on the court. Whenever I watched them play, it felt like I witnessed a cultural melting pot on the basketball court.

Whether it was Jordan's aerial acrobatics or Ming's finesse in the low post, NBA players had several qualities that set them apart from their mediocre counterparts:

NBA QUALITIES

- **Optimism**: The NBA's true hardcourt warriors never flinched during critical moments of their careers – they remained positive even if the odds were stacked against them. The eighth-seeded Denver Nuggets' upset of the top-seeded Seattle Supersonics in the 1994 NBA playoffs quickly comes to mind. Although Shawn Kemp's Sonics had a 2-0 series lead, the Nuggets remained positive. Dikembe Mutombo and co. won the next three games to pull off one of the greatest upsets in NBA history.

- **Resiliency**: Many NBA players never quit during trying times on the hardcourt. Isiah Thomas's 25-point outburst against the Lakers in the 1988 NBA Finals was a prime example. Willis Reed's valiant performance despite a serious thigh injury in game seven of the 1970 NBA Finals was another one. When basketball players make it to the professional ranks, the NBA will test their mettle at some point during their careers.

- **Killer instinct**: This applies to NBA players who consistently exceed expectations during crunch time (the waning moments of a game when the outcome hangs in the balance). Indiana Pacers legend Reggie Miller was a player who showed killer instinct many times during his Hall of Fame career.

    Miller did the unthinkable in the 1995 NBA playoffs when he scored eight points in nine seconds (six points from two three-pointers and two from two free throws) in the fourth quarter to beat the Pacers' rivals, the New York Knicks. That's the perfect example of killer instinct at basketball's highest level.

Players who exemplify these traits consistently during their NBA careers have a good chance of entering the Naismith Memorial Basketball Hall of Fame in Springfield, MA. It's considered the holy grail of basketball – an elite group of players who not only broke various basketball-related records but also set the gold standard on how succeeding generations should play the game.

The Naismith Memorial Basketball Hall of Fame mentions the eligibility requirements for various induction categories on its official website:

- **Player**: A player must have been retired for four full seasons for consideration. The earliest he or she can merit consideration is in his or her fifth year of retirement. If, for some reason, the player decides to play again, the Screening Committee will review his or her case accordingly.
- **Coach**: A coach under consideration should have been retired for four full seasons prior to induction. If he or she is still active, he or she must have coached at the high school, college, or pro levels for at least twenty-five years. He or she can merit consideration on his or her sixth year of retirement or twenty-sixth year of full-time coaching.
- **Referee**: The consideration for referees is similar to the criteria for retired and active coaches.
- **Contributor**: If an individual makes a 'significant contribution' (a distinction the Hall's Election Process Committee and Contributor Direct-Elect Committee determines), he or she can earn enshrinement at any time.

In terms of the election process, the president and CEO of the Naismith Memorial Basketball Hall of Fame receives completed nomination forms on October 31st every year. These completed nomination forms become part of the official ballots that are subject to committee review.

Here are some quotations from Hall of Fame players and coaches to inspire you:

- "I've failed over and over again in my life. And that's why I succeed." – Michael Jordan
- "If you run into a wall, don't turn around and give up. Figure out how to climb it." – Michael Jordan
- "I can accept failure – everyone fails at something. But I can't accept not trying." – Michael Jordan
- "I have nothing in common with lazy people who blame others for their lack of success." – Kobe Bryant
- "If you see me in a fight with a bear, pray for the bear." – Kobe Bryant
- "Failing to prepare is preparing to fail." – John Wooden
- "The only person who can really motivate you is you." – Shaquille O'Neal
- "Good, better, best. Never let it rest until your good is better and your better is best." – Tim Duncan
- "You don't have to be Magic to be special. You're already special – you're you." – Magic Johnson
- "Confidence is everything in this game. If you don't think you can, you won't." – Jerry West

Whether a player is Hall-of-Fame worthy or not, their personal life is always under the spotlight – many fans want to know about these hardcourt heroes' daily lives. Some of these players have strong family ties, while some come from humble beginnings, poverty, and broken families.

Regardless of their backgrounds, players follow a rigid schedule during the NBA season. For instance, a typical game-day schedule looks like this:

1. Wake up at 6:00 a.m.

2. Do strength training from 6:15 a.m. to 7:45 a.m.
3. Eat breakfast at 8:30 a.m.
4. Complete various basketball-related drills until 10:30 a.m.
5. Rest for an hour
6. Work on shooting from 11:30 a.m. to 1 p.m.
7. Eat lunch at 1 p.m.
8. Afternoon nap
9. Game-day preparations several hours before tip-off at 7 p.m.

It's an unforgiving and relentless schedule, considering players sometimes play back-to-back games and don't arrive in another city until the wee hours of the morning. The eighty-two-game NBA schedule is a grind, to say the least.

Despite the players' unrelenting day-to-day schedule, many of them take their roles in the community seriously. Big-name players, such as four-time NBA MVP LeBron James of the Los Angeles Lakers, give back to the less fortunate. James, the NBA's all-time scoring leader (38,652 points prior to the 2023-24 NBA season), spearheads various at-risk-youth charities via his LeBron James Family Foundation.

On the flip side, some big-name players get themselves in trouble on and off the court. For example, the Memphis Grizzlies suspended their star point guard Ja Morant from all team activities in May 2023 after he allegedly brandished a handgun while singing rap tunes on a passenger seat during an Instagram Live session that month.

Morant, a 6'2" two-time NBA All-Star who isn't afraid to dunk against bigger competition, tarnished his reputation in the process. Paul Pierce, the retired Boston Celtic forward, also fell out of favor with the public after he went live on social media with several women dancing in the background during a party.

Consequently, ESPN fired him from his job as an NBA analyst in 2021. This turn of events isn't surprising considering ESPN is a Disney company that doesn't tolerate outlandish behavior from its employees.

I think it's a shame – many youngsters look up to NBA players as role models. All it takes is one misstep or foolish decision to jeopardize their once-promising careers. It's nothing new, after all – former Chicago Bulls forward Dennis Rodman had a lengthy arrest record for assault and DUI during his playing days in the 1990s.

Unfortunately, the trend has continued to the present day. NBA players' shenanigans can become trending topics on Twitter and make headlines on TMZ Sports in an instant.

Here's the key takeaway: players' private lives have a profound impact on their NBA careers. Legions of LeBron fans consider him not only one of the greatest to lace up a pair of sneakers but also one of the most charitable NBA superstars in league history.

For their parts, Morant, Pierce, and Rodman must live with the consequences of their actions. Although they made plenty of highlights on ESPN's SportsCenter, their tarnished legacies might haunt them for the rest of their lives.

With that in mind, let's delve deeper into fascinating basketball stories that include the game's invention, the creation of the NBA, injuries, the evolution of NBA jerseys, and many more. Each story includes various subplots about strength, perseverance, and triumph that will intrigue and inspire you.

I will also include other, lesser-known stories such as former gang members becoming NBA stars, and black athletes enduring racial discrimination on the court. Buckle up, because this is going to be one of the most entertaining rides of your life.

And if you enjoy the book, I would love it if you can leave an honest review on amazon; this helps other readers discover it and enjoy it too.

Chapter 1:
THE BIRTH OF BASKETBALL

"The invention of basketball was not an accident. It was developed to meet a need. Those boys would simply not play 'Drop the Handkerchief.'"
– James Naismith

Who would've thought a Canadian would invent a game that would become popular in the United States?

That's exactly what happened on December 12, 1891, when James Naismith, a native of Almonte, Canada West, and a full-time instructor at the YMCA of Springfield, MA, came up with an idea. Naismith had a dilemma: he had to think of a way to cope with his restless and unruly students who were cooped up at the YMCA on a cold and blustery day. They remained restless despite playing a makeshift indoor football game. Naismith had to think of something – and fast.

Naismith thought long term: he wanted to invent a game that would keep his students preoccupied during the harsh winter months in the frigid Northeast region. Before long, the thirty-year-old Naismith made up a sport that combined the facets of rugby, lacrosse, and a childhood game, 'Duck on a Rock.'

Naismith cleared the gym's wooden floor, scooped up a soccer ball, and asked the custodian for two square boxes. Unfortunately, the latter could only provide him with two peach baskets. Naismith had no choice but to improvise – he took the two peach baskets and attached them to the gym's two balcony rails. The baskets hung ten feet from the YMCA's wooden floor.

Some forty-eight years later, during a radio interview at New York City's WOR-AM, Naismith said he split the boys into two groups of nine players. He told them the objective of the game was to shoot the soccer ball into the peach baskets. The first basketball game in history was officially underway.

Since basketball was a brand-new sport, the boys were still learning the ropes and playing with reckless abandon – they tackled, kicked, and punched their opponents at will. It hardly resembled the game millions of basketball fans love today – it resembled a bloody team combat sport that made Naismith scratch his head.

Nevertheless, the boys loved Naismith's new game. They loved it so much that they pestered him to play again. Naismith obliged. However, this time around, he had to formulate new rules to make the game safer and more enjoyable for the players.

Naismith promptly summed up late 19th century basketball in thirteen rules that his secretary typed in two pages:

1. Players can throw the ball in any direction with one or two hands.
2. Players can fight for ball possession with one or two hands.
3. Running with the ball is not allowed. Players must pass the ball from the spot on the court where they caught it.
4. Only the players' hands – not the arms or body – can hold the ball.
5. Physical contact, such as shoving, tripping, and holding, is not allowed. Should a player commit a similar infraction, the official called him for a foul. A second infraction means disqualification from the game.
6. Striking the ball with a fist also counts as a foul.
7. If a team commits three consecutive fouls, their opponent earns a goal.

8. A scoring attempt counts as a goal when the ball remains in the peach basket.
9. If the ball goes out of bounds, a player from the team that retained possession has five seconds to get the ball into play. If he takes longer than five seconds to throw the ball inbounds, the opponents regain possession.
10. Umpires inform the referee whenever players commit fouls.
11. For his part, the referee determines where the ball is in play and which team earns possession of the ball. He also keeps track of the game's duration.
12. The game has two fifteen-minute halves with a five-minute break after the first half.
13. The team that scores the most goals after thirty minutes of play is the winner. If there is a tie after two halves, the teams keep playing until one side scores the winning goal.

News of Naismith's brilliant creation spread like wildfire at other YMCA branches and college campuses. Basketball became one of the fastest-growing sports of his era. Better yet, it appealed to a huge audience – even women dressed up in blouses played the game in the late 19th century.

Naismith's athletics career took off several years after he invented basketball. The Kansas Jayhawks – an eventual basketball powerhouse in the NCAA ranks – made Naismith their first head men's basketball coach in 1898.

While Naismith was calling the shots for the Jayhawks, basketball evolved dramatically. Game administrators eventually cut the bottoms off the peach baskets to make it easier to retrieve the balls. Naismith also whittled down the number of players on the court from nine to five. Shooting free throws and dribbling the basketball followed suit at the turn of the twentieth century. Naismith's original thirteen rules are currently preserved at the University of Kansas.

Basketball continued gaining serious traction in the twentieth century. Many major colleges already had basketball varsity teams in 1900. The

IN THE GAME

National Collegiate Athletics Association (NCAA) began overseeing college basketball nine years later. The inaugural NCAA Division I Tournament (which eventually became known as 'March Madness') took place in 1939.

Basketball became so popular, it made its debut in the Summer Olympics in Berlin, Germany in 1936. Naismith himself tossed the basketball for the inaugural tip-off. He also presented the medals to the competitors after the United States beat Canada in the gold medal match, 19-8. James Naismith's name transcended international borders almost fifty years after he invented basketball.

Not only that, but the game also reached unprecedented heights several years after the end of World War II.

The National Basketball Association (NBA) was born in 1949. It has represented the highest level of professional basketball for the past seventy-four years. While the NBA gained momentum over the years, basketball became a global game – various professional leagues sprouted in Turkey, China, Spain, Italy, Australia, France, and South America. To make a long story short, basketball has become a bona fide global game. And it all started with the ingenuity of a Canadian YMCA instructor named James Naismith.

Who would have thought a game that featured two peach baskets would eventually snowball to become one of the most popular games in the world? Basketball's massive appeal is evident whenever fans wear their favorite player's jersey and when people assemble basketball hoops in their front yard. Naismith's creativity paved the way for a global phenomenon that has made headlines for years on end. Little wonder the Naismith Memorial Basketball Hall of Fame (he was inducted in 1959) carries his famous name.

Although basketball appeals to players of different ages and nationalities, little do they know their predecessors once showcased their talents in settings that were more appropriate for wrestlers such as Hulk Hogan, The Ultimate Warrior, Stone Cold Steve Austin, Razor Ramon, and Shawn Michaels.

Here's a hint: the unusual setting gave birth to contemporary basketball players' famous moniker.

Chapter 2:
WHEN THE COURT WAS A CAGE

It isn't just the game of basketball that has evolved dramatically over the years. Collective nicknames for players have also evolved in recent memory.

For instance, fans and the media refer to basketball players as 'hoopsters' – a reference to the hoop used for scoring points on the hardcourt. People also often refer to basketball players as 'ballers.'

Not only is 'baller' a catchy nickname, but it's also one of the best compliments you can pay a basketball player. Guys such as LeBron James of the Los Angeles Lakers, Jayson Tatum of the Boston Celtics, Jimmy Butler of the Miami Heat, Zach Lavine of the Chicago Bulls, and Tyrese Haliburton of the Indiana Pacers are 'ballers' – they're perennial All-Stars and some of the best players in the NBA. If you compete against a top-notch player in the playground, he's a 'baller' because he sets the bar high every time he plays.

If you play basketball, do you want people to call you a 'hoopster' or 'baller?' Can you imagine people calling you a 'cager?'

That's right – fans and media also refer to basketball players as 'cagers.' The unusual moniker stemmed from the setting of the first professional basketball game at a social hall in Trenton, NJ in 1896. Just five years after James Naismith put up two peach baskets for his students at the Springfield

IN THE GAME

YMCA, the game of basketball saw an innovation that would make today's fans scratch their heads.

In the early days of basketball, fights were commonplace, along with myriad other disturbances: fans lobbed produce onto the court; if a ball went into the crowd, it became a souvenir (much like in baseball); the rules at the time stated that the player who got to an out-of-bounds ball first would retain possession, which led to plenty of diving into spectators, and other slowdowns in play.

Organizers assembled a twelve-foot cage with wire-mesh fencing that surrounded the court's perimeter. At first glance, the setup would remind today's fans of the World Wrestling Entertainment (WWE) cage matches where protagonists such as Hulk Hogan or Stone Cold Steve Austin beat each other up before one of them climbed the cage, stepped out, and won the match to the delight of their delirious fans.

Surprisingly, a basketball cage match had some impressive benefits. For one, the cages protected the fans. If you watch highlights of scrappy NBA players such as Dennis Rodman, Jeff Foster, or Udonis Haslem diving for loose balls with reckless abandon on YouTube, there's a good chance they will run over some fans in the stands.

That scenario wasn't possible with a cage installed around the court's perimeter in the late 19th century. If you were alive back then, you could grab a courtside seat without worrying about a seven-footer plowing into you at full speed. Think Shaqulle O'Neal and all 325 pounds of him crushing you under his weight!

Basketball cages had other impressive benefits: they also protected the players and decreased the chances of career-threatening injuries. Albert Cooper, Jr., a player of Naismith's era, shared his thoughts on basketball cages in 1991 (via *Sports Illustrated* and *Sportskeeda*):

"I played in cages up to 1929 when they stopped using them in Trenton. When they eliminated the cages, I never cared for basketball after that."

"All of the basketball players in those days enjoyed playing in a cage because there was less chance of injury than there is today. You learned how

to protect yourself. If you got jammed against the cage, it didn't bother you."

Joel S. Gotthoffer, another cager of that era, discussed basketball's violent nature back then:

"I played the first few games at (Nanticoke) in a rope cage, and I came home with the cage's markings on me. You could play tic-tac-toe on everybody after a game because the cage marked you up; sometimes you were bleeding and sometimes you were not. You were like a gladiator, and if you didn't get rid of the ball, you could get killed."

The cages also protected the players from irate fans. Opponents typically wanted to drive the ball-carrier into the protective netting. The poor fellow suffered a double whammy: the opposition clobbered him and he also sent several fans toppling over like dominoes. Some fans didn't let that slide – they put up their dukes to get a piece of the offending player. Sometimes, they even went too far by entering the basketball cage doors and pummeling the guilty party.

Basketball cages weren't just about safety. According to a 1991 featured article on *Sports Illustrated* commemorating basketball's hundredth anniversary, the cages made the game more fun and entertaining because it didn't take long for players to get the ball back into play (later known as inbounding the ball). Plus, the ball and players could bounce off the wire mesh (which was later changed to rope netting) similar to Hogan, Austin, and their other wrestling contemporaries.

As more professional leagues in the United States' northeast region used basketball cages in the late 19th century until the 1930s, they became known as 'cagers' for obvious reasons. The term only applied to pros, because high school and college players never used basketball cages back in the day.

Professional leagues that used basketball cages drew large crowds. In fact, the Cleveland Rosenblums often drew an average attendance of 10,000 fans for their weekend games in the 1920s, according to *Sports Illustrated*.

That trend inspired the founders of the American Basketball League (ABL) to establish their own pro basketball league in 1925. The ABL, which featured teams from Washington, D.C., New York, Boston, Chicago, and Fort Wayne, IN, adopted amateur rules and disallowed the double dribble (a ball handling violation where the player dribbles the ball simultaneously with both hands) and basketball cages.

Although the ABL folded during the height of the Great Depression in 1931, it marked a crucial transition in basketball history. Basketball cages became obsolete after that. Cages lost their appeal because tournament organizers used them mainly in the Northeast region. Basketball tournaments in other states didn't use them. Cages also became an occupational hazard for the players – some cagers such as Philadelphia Sphas star Joel S. Gotthoffer went home bleeding with cage markings on their bodies. Gotthoffer compared the experience to the Roman gladiator era. If players could not get rid of the ball in time, they would get hit and put their lives at risk. Although the basketball cage lost its appeal as the world ushered in the 1920s, the nickname 'cagers' for basketball players has stuck around to the present day.

While playing basketball in cages during the game's first forty years of existence helped protect fans and players from melees and fights to a certain degree, brawls and fisticuffs have always been a part of basketball history.

Since emotions run high and tempers flare during a basketball game, brawls can happen at any moment, especially if an opponent gets under a player's skin. Once a player throws the first punch, it sets off a domino effect that can lead to hefty suspensions and fines and this happened frequently.

In the next chapter, we will talk about the legendary Suns and how they introduced the modern style.

Chapter 3:
SEVEN SECONDS OR LESS: HOW THE SUNS INTRODUCED THE MODERN STYLE

By 2005, fans were witnessing a different NBA than they were used to. Offense was stagnant. Scoring was down. Teams used to regularly score in the 100s, whereas now there were games in the 80s. Even that year's Finals, which went the full seven games, was unsatisfactory.

The San Antonio Spurs beat the Detroit Pistons at home, winning their third championship since 1999. The final score of that deciding contest? 81-74.

Few knew it at the time, but there was a revolutionary change coming in the desert. The Phoenix Suns would never win a championship, but their style changed the course of offensive tactics for years to come, and its influence continues to this day.

The architect of this legendary style was Mike D'Antoni, who was promoted from assistant to head coach in 2003, winning 21 games against 40 losses in the '03-'04 season. At that time, the Suns were a disjointed bunch, without direction. D'Antoni had an idea for a fast-paced system, which required a point guard capable of taking the proverbial steering wheel.

That's when they signed Steve Nash in free agency, and everything changed. With the Dallas Mavericks, Nash thrived in an up-tempo offense. Thus, D'Antoni saw him as the perfect leader to execute his bold basketball vision.

The roster already had promise, with budding stars Amar'e Stoudemire, Shawn Marion, Quentin Richardson, and Joe Johnson. Now, with a floor general like Nash, the talents around him could flourish. In their first year together, they compiled the league's best regular-season mark at 62-20 and had the best offensive rating since the 72-win Chicago Bulls of 1995-96.

Nash and Stoudemire emerged as an unstoppable one-two offensive combination, especially with their execution of the pick-and-roll. While most teams were averaging under 12 three-point tries per **game**, Richardson alone averaged eight. Another key to their offense was their versatility. Stoudemire was tall, but able to take jumpers. Johnson could play the point or small forward. Marion had the capability to move to any of the five positions on defense.

But the calling card of this team was their speed. They called it the "Seven Seconds or Less' offense, because of how briefly each possession lasted. D'Antoni's philosophy was centered on getting a good shot as quickly as possible.

This was in stark contrast to the title teams in the 2000s, which featured dominant centers like Shaquille O'Neal of the Lakers and Tim Duncan of the Spurs. Instead of being deliberate and utilizing a plodding half-court game, the Suns were improvisational. The shot clock was unimportant. They wore out opposing defenses with a veritable track meet of fast-paced maneuvers. For fans, it was a pleasant diversion – reminiscent of the "Showtime" offense that the Los Angeles Lakers rode to great success in the 1980s.

The Suns were the fastest team by far, made more threes than any team had ever made in a season, and, in the 2004-05 season, improved by thirty-three victories over the previous year. It was the third-greatest single-season turnaround in NBA history at the time. D'Antoni was named

Coach of the Year. Nash was named league MVP (and would win again the next year).

These Suns made it all the way to the Western Conference Finals but couldn't get past the San Antonio Spurs. The tortoise beat the hare and won in five games.

Despite a few personnel changes, including the loss of Stoudamire to injury, the style never wavered in 2005-06. The Suns won 54 games and were again a step away from the NBA Finals following a pair of thrilling series triumphs over the Lakers and Clippers.

This time it was the Mavericks who knocked out Phoenix – winning in six.

In retrospect, the 2006-07 season was the Suns' best chance. They went 61-21 and scored 3.2 more points per 100 possessions than any other team. The top-seeded Mavericks were eliminated in the first round by the Golden State Warriors. The East was mediocre at best. The door was wide open for Phoenix to push though.

It was in this playoff run that the flashpoint moment of this era occurred. In the last moments of Game 4, the Suns were about to tie the Spurs in their conference semifinal series, before Robert Horry delivered a hip check to Nash that sent the MVP into the scorers table.

Nash would be uninjured. But Stoudemire and Boris Diaw, who were out of the game, went over to check on their teammate. Since leaving the bench in such a situation is disallowed, NBA commissioner David Stern suspended them both for Game 5 – a game the Spurs won. San Antonio took Game 6 as well.

It would be as close as these Suns would ever get. But while Phoenix ultimately came up short, its scheme has evolved over time, and became the backbone for the champions to follow.

Teams looked to not only run but shoot threes. Organizations were less inclined for the 'big man' in the middle and more apt to take a swing option who could excel in the paint, driving to the hoop, or spotting up for a jumper.

IN THE GAME

Pace-and-space and spread pick-and-roll systems became the bedrock of modern NBA offense. To watch the NBA today is to watch the ripple effects of what the Suns created.

All styles inevitably evolve, and the 'Seven Seconds or Less' style morphed into a perimeter-heavy approach. Teams discovered the efficiency of the three-point shot relative to long two-point attempts. In 2004-05, the average number of threes per game was 15.8. From there began an increased progression. No team better embraced this style, and used it to tremendous success, than the Golden State Warriors.

In 2015, led by head coach Steve Kerr, the Warriors won the NBA title, connecting on 10.9 from beyond the arc during the regular season. It would be the first of four rings – the latest of those coming in 2022.

Of course, it helps to have the right players. And in 2009, the Warriors drafted an all-timer with the seventh overall pick: Steph Curry from Davidson.

His shooting efficiency from beyond the three-point line, and his versatility shooting off-the-dribble or in-motion, has made him a singular offensive talent. Additional personnel changes sought to leverage this uncanny ability.

In 2011, the Warriors drafted Klay Thompson – another three-point shooting ace, and an excellent perimeter defender. The next year, they drafted forward Draymond Green in the second round, who added tremendous value in his passing and rebounding.

Led by this trio, Golden State made consecutive playoff appearances in 2013 and 2014. Mark Jackson was replaced by Kerr, and his motion offense sent the Warriors into the stratosphere.

In Kerr's first year at the helm, Golden State went 67-15 (the best mark in franchise history) and its 39.8 percent rate from three was the best in the NBA. Curry won his first MVP and the Warriors defeated the LeBron James-led Cavaliers in the Finals.

The next year was arguably the greatest regular season ever. Golden State, behind another MVP year from Curry, won an NBA record seventy-three games. But they couldn't win the one that counts most. In a rematch with the Cavs, the Warriors let a 3-1 series lead vanish. Ultimately, Cleveland won in a dramatic seventh game.

The Warriors answered that defeat by improving their roster immensely with the addition of Kevin Durant. Already one of the game's greatest players, Durant was a star who was without a ring. He played in Golden State only three years, but made three Finals appearances, won two titles, and claimed two Finals MVP Awards. The one year Durant didn't win, he suffered a devastating Achilles tendon tear in Game 5 in what would be a six-game defeat by the Toronto Raptors.

Durant's departure led to a couple of rough years for the Warriors in which they missed the playoffs, only to answer back emphatically with their fourth title run – culminating in a series win over Boston.

The emergence of the Golden State Warriors as the most dominant team in the NBA would prompt every team in both the Eastern and Western Conferences to search for and cultivate three-point shooting talent in an effort to compete with the Warriors. It has now become a fixture of the league. During the 2021-22 season, the average number of three-pointers attempted was 35.2, the highest total in league history.

While the Warriors are the modern-day dynasty, the Boston Celtics were the dominant team in the late 1950s and through the 1960s. The most significant player of that Celtics team is also one of the most influential figures in basketball history, Bill Russell, who we will talk about in the next chapter.

Chapter 4:
THE LEGACY OF BILL RUSSELL

Up until the very end of his playing career, he was a winner. There was little reason for the Boston Celtics to beat the Los Angeles Lakers in Game 7 of the 1969 NBA Finals. Sure, the Celtics had defeated the Lakers six times before in the championship round. The Lakers were younger and boasted more talent. They had Wilt Chamberlain, the most dominant player of his era, who joined the Lakers prior to the 1968-69 campaign.

They had Jerry West and Elgin Baylor, two veterans who had been a part of each championship series defeat and two of the greatest to ever suit up.

Los Angeles had the better players, but Boston had the better team.

It's hard to imagine anyone representing the importance of the collective more than Bill Russell.

His leadership went beyond starting at center for the Celtics; he was a player-coach. It had been his role since 1966 when he took over for the legendary Red Auerbach. When they won the 1968 Finals, Russell became the first black head coach to win an NBA title.

In 1969, a weary Celtics club pulled itself together and got to the championship round for the 12th time in Russell's career. Before the start of the seventh and deciding contest at the Los Angeles Forum, even Lakers owner

Jack Kent Cooke was convinced Boston didn't have a chance to beat his club. He had thousands of balloons with "World Champion Lakers" printed on them suspended from the rafters, among other festivities.

The Celtics, though, took a 15-point lead into the fourth quarter. Los Angeles came back and cut the lead to one with under two minutes remaining. Boston had possession and a loose ball went right to Don Nelson, who put up a desperation 18-footer from the free throw line to beat the shot clock. The ball hit the back rim, bounced high in the air and fell through the hoop. It gave the Celtics a three-point lead they wouldn't relinquish.

Being interviewed on television in the locker room, Russell could barely muster a response. It was to be his last true association with the Celtics. He left his posts as center and head coach.

The legacy of Bill Russell in Boston, for those only familiar with the on-court achievements, is beyond remarkable: eleven NBA titles in a thirteen-year span, including eight in a row. A defensive presence like no other. The greatest winner in sports history.

But a broader look at Russell beyond the basketball court – as a social justice advocate and a pioneer – is much more complex.

Russell initially grew up in West Monroe, Louisiana. As was typical of the south, the town was segregated, and the family dealt regularly with prejudice. They moved to Oakland, California, when he was eight. Russell developed a close bond with his mother, who passed away when he was just twelve. Russell began to learn the game at a young age, but his skills were far from developed even as he left high school.

He was ignored by most college scouts mainly because he wasn't a starter in high school. He lacked fundamentals, but had a sense for the game and the moment. It took very little time for him to make an impact. In his first eligible season, Russell scored 19.9 points per game and averaged 19.2 rebounds. It's unknown how many blocks he had since those weren't recorded at the time, but a rule change from the NCAA in which the lane was widened—reportedly in response to Russell's dominance—speaks to his prowess as a defender.

IN THE GAME

In addition to helping San Francisco run through the NCAA Tournament unscathed in his last two seasons, he also was part of a club that reeled off fifty-five consecutive victories. Russell's ability as a clutch performer was also evident, as he put up 23 points and 25 rebounds in his first Finals appearance against Tom Gola and LaSalle and 26 points and 27 rebounds the following year versus Iowa.

Russell won everywhere he played – in college, in the pros, and as an Olympian in 1956.

His Celtics career began thanks to an unusual series of events on draft day. The Saint Louis Hawks swapped the second pick with Boston because they were given Ed Macauley, who had asked to be traded close to home because of his son suffering from cerebral palsy, and Cliff Hagan.

Boston agreed and a dynasty was born.

Russell wore Celtic green from 1956 through 1969. Only twice did he not play for the NBA title. While the efforts of many helped to forge this powerhouse – including guard extraordinaire Bob Cousy, Tom Heinsohn, John Havlicek, and Sam Jones – Russell was the focal point.

The key was his presence in the paint – as a dominant defender and unstoppable force on the boards. Russell continued to improve his shot-blocking ability and rebounding skills. He fundamentally changed the way defense was played, and revolutionized the role of the big man. His skill at taking in a missed shot ignited the Celtics' vaunted fast-break offense.

Beyond any on-court statistics, Russell was the consummate leader. He elevated the play of his teammates through his unselfishness, determination, and basketball intelligence. He was immensely respected by fellow players, coaches, and fans.

In what would be an inspiration to future athletes, Russell used his platform to advocate for civil rights and social justice causes. He boycotted a game in Lexington, Kentucky, in 1961 because the hotel he and his black teammates were supposed to stay in wouldn't accommodate them.

As a black athlete playing in a racially divided United States, Russell himself faced significant challenges and discrimination – this even happened in Boston, which created a rift with the city long after he retired. Nonetheless, he became a trailblazer for racial equality in professional sports, challenging stereotypes and inspiring discourse.

Russell actively participated in civil rights marches and protests during the 1960s, including the March on Washington for Jobs and Freedom in 1963, where Martin Luther King Jr. delivered his famous "I Have a Dream" speech. His contributions to the Civil Rights Movement were significant.

Russell's activism had a lasting impact. He paved the way for future generations of athletes to speak out on social and political issues. His efforts helped to highlight the importance of using one's platform for positive change, demonstrating the power of athletes to influence social reform beyond the realm of sports, and inspiring others to do the same.

Bill Russell's impact on the Boston Celtics and the sport of basketball endured after his number 6 was retired, first after his Basketball Hall of Fame induction in 1975, when it was retired from the Celtics, and then after his passing in 2022, when it became the first number to be retired across the entire NBA.

He succeeded, and expanded on the dreams of, those from generations before him who were considered the first hoopers. Lets get into that in the next chapter.

Chapter 5:
THE FIRST HOOPERS

Who would've thought that eighteen rowdy and restless college-age kids would become the first basketball players in history?

Those boys were so restless, boisterous, and disorderly, they made two instructors at the YMCA in Springfield, MA, quit. Little did they know that their replacement, a Canadian named James Naismith, would not only straighten them out but also make them pioneers of a game millions of people would come to love.

When Naismith put up two peach baskets and told his students to play "basket ball" (that was what he called the game at the time) on December 21st, 1891, the boys had second thoughts – they had never seen anything like it. However, they eventually relented and played enthusiastically. According to the Naismith Memorial Basketball Hall of Fame's official website, Naismith did what no other instructor at the Springfield YMCA had previously done – make the boys play with that kind of enthusiasm and passion.

So, the first basketball players were born. There were nine players on each team and eighteen players in all. Here are the names of the first hoopers in basketball history:

FIRST HOOPERS

- Lyman W. Archibald
- Franklin E. Barnes
- Wilbert F. Carey
- William R. Chase
- William H. Davis
- George E. Day
- Benjamin S. French
- Henri Gelan
- Ernest G. Hildner
- Genzaburo Ishikawa
- Raymond P. Kaighn
- Eugene S. Libby
- Findley G. MacDonald
- Frank Mahan
- T. Duncan Patton
- Edwin P. Ruggles
- John G. Thompson
- George R. Weller

Naismith implemented his thirteen rules for basketball just several weeks later. The game evolved into the professional level, where players showcased their diverse talents in high-wire mesh fences and cages in 1896, a trend that continued until the early 1930s.

Some fifteen years later, hockey arena owners in the U.S. and Canada formed the Basketball Association of America (BAA). It eventually merged with the NBL to form the National Basketball Association (NBA) in 1949.

IN THE GAME

Prior to these events, several basketball players stood out from their contemporaries during World War II. These old-time hoopers raised the bar high and set the standard for future hardcourt heroes:

WORLD WAR II HOOPERS

- **Gene Englund**: Englund was a 6'5" forward/center (he was small for a center by today's standards – many modern centers stand at least 7' tall) who attended the University of Wisconsin. Englund, a former Big Ten MVP, joined the National Basketball League (NBL) in 1941. He spent a combined seven seasons with the NBL's Oshkosh All-Stars from 1941 to 1949. He also suited up for the American Basketball League's (ABL) Brooklyn Indians during that eight-year time frame.

  Englund led the All-Stars to the NBL title as a rookie during the 1941-42 season. When the NBL folded in 1949, Englund's 380 points were the third-highest accrued in league history. The *thirty-two-year-old* forward became a pioneer member of the NBA's Boston Celtics that same year. He averaged 8.2 points in twenty-four career games for the Celtics. He played his final NBA season with the Tri-Cities Blackhawks (now known as the Atlanta Hawks) in 1950.

- **Leroy Edwards**: Edwards was one of the first dominant, big men in professional basketball history. Not only that, but he also became the first known hooper to leave college early (he played for the Kentucky Wildcats men's basketball team) and turn professional – a move that was unheard of at the time. It wasn't until more than fifty years later when players such as Allen Iverson, Carmelo Anthony, DeMar DeRozan, Chris Bosh, Victor Oladipo, and Bradley Beal made leaving college early the norm for some future NBA stars.

  For his part, Edwards left Kentucky after his sophomore season to play for the NBL's Oshkosh All-Stars. It was a risk that paid off for the young Edwards: he became one of the league's prominent low-post scorers who could shoot a hook shot (a shot whose trajectory resembles that of a hook) with either hand. He eventually led the

NBL in scoring three times and became a six-time First-Team All-League selection. Edwards retired in the years leading up to the historic BAA-NBL merger in 1949.

- **Bobby McDermott**: McDermott was a Brooklyn playground legend who caught the eye of the Metropolitan Basketball League's Brooklyn Visitations. He was so good that the Visitations signed him immediately after he dropped out of high school after just one year of attendance.

  McDermott was a guard, known for his two-handed set shot (a shot a player shoots with two hands from chest level). He led the Ft. Wayne Zollner Pistons (now known as the Detroit Pistons) to two straight NBL titles in 1944 and 1945. Behind the exploits of McDermott and big man George Mikan, the Chicago American Gears won the NBA title in 1947. McDermott's prolific professional basketball career included stints with the Baltimore Clippers, Sheboygan Red Skins, Tri-Cities Blackhawks, Hammond Calumet Buccaneers, Wiles-Barre Barons, and Grand Rapids Hornets. He was also a player-coach for the Pistons ('43-'45, then again in '47), Gears ('47), Red Skins ('47-'48), Blackhawks ('48-'49), and Hornets ('50).

- **Mel Riebe**: Riebe was a 5'11" guard who paved the way for high-scoring guards in the NBA such as Allen Iverson, Isiah Thomas, Dwyane Wade, Anfernee "Penny" Hardaway, Ja Morant, DeAaron Fox, and Tyrese Haliburton.

  Riebe averaged a 17.9 points for the Cleveland Chase Brassmen in the 1943-1944 NBL season. He proved his showing was no fluke when he averaged an incredible 20.2 points per game for the Cleveland Ailmen Transfers one year later. Riebe, a two-time NBL scoring leader, set the bar high for guards of his era. If he played in the modern NBA, he would have given Iverson, Morant, and Wade stiff competition. Watching Riebe score at will, shooting a two-handed set shot from the 1940s against those guys would be amusing, to say the least.

Riebe was also a rare breed of athlete. He also played minor league baseball for his hometown Cleveland Indians during his illustrious NBL career. Consequently, he became one of the first dual-sport athletes of the 1940s. It's an incredible accomplishment considering legendary Chicago Bulls guard Michael Jordan played minor league baseball from 1993 to 1994, but performed poorly. No matter how good a basketball player is, attempting a foray into another sport like baseball is another story. Mel Riebe was one of the few to ever pull it off.

Notice that players from the 1940s did not score as many points as their successors, because there was no shot clock (teams are given twenty-four seconds to score whenever they have the ball; otherwise, they commit a shot-clock violation and turn the ball over to their opponents) during their era. It wasn't until 1954 that the NBA made the shot clock an official part of the game.

Nevertheless, players such as Englund, Edwards, McDermott, and Riebe stood out not only because of their athleticism, but also because of their feel for the game. They could shoot hook shots and two-handed set shots far better than other players of the 1940s. Although they weren't physically imposing, they performed better because their passion for basketball was innate. The game felt like second nature to them.

Wouldn't it be interesting to see modern ballers play a similar throwback style in today's NBA? Kareem Abdul-Jabbar's hook shot was the closest thing in contemporary basketball to the NBA of the late 1940s. Nobody could block that shot. Abdul-Jabbar went on to score 38,387 points (second-highest scoring in NBA history as of this writing), mostly with his patented hook shot.

Abdul-Jabbar was one of the greatest players in Los Angeles Lakers franchise history. We will delve further into how another Lakers legend became part of the NBA's logo in the next chapter.

Chapter 6:
THE ICONIC NBA LOGO

Have you ever wondered who's behind the famous silhouette in the NBA logo?

To be completely honest, I had no idea who that player was when I was an awkward and gangly teen basketball fan. It wasn't until much later when I found who that mysterious player was – Jerry West.

Yes, it's Jerry West, the sharpshooting guard who played for the Los Angeles Lakers from 1960 to 1974 who became the symbol of the National Basketball Association more than fifty years ago.

NBA commissioner J. Walter Kennedy tapped sports brand consultant Alan Siegel to redesign the NBA's logo toward the end of the 1960s. Siegel was the same consultant who oversaw Jerry Dior's creation of the Major League Baseball (MLB) logo in 1968.

Sigel told ANDSCAPE's Aaron Dodson in 2017 that he gained access to *SPORT* magazine's photo database courtesy of his good friend and legendary sportswriter Dick Schaap. Siegel rummaged through the photos and thought one that showed West dribbling toward the basket was the most appealing:

"I went through the files and found a number of images of NBA players. I found an image of Jerry West, which is what I used as the basis of the

logo. I was attracted to it because it was nice and vertical, and it had him leaning and dribbling – had a little motion to it.

"I designed eight, nine or ten different versions, and that turned out to be the most effective. I presented it to the NBA and they approved it immediately and began to use it."

Siegel considered some images of Kareem Abdul-Jabbar, Wilt Chamberlain, Tom Havlicek, and Tom Gola but thought West's photo stood out. West was already an established NBA star when his silhouette became an integral part of the NBA logo in 1969. He had earned nine NBA All-Star and six All-NBA First-Team selections when he entered his tenth professional season that year.

Apparently, West never wanted to become the face of the NBA. Siegel told Dodson he first met West while the retired Lakers great was having lunch in the late 1990s. When West found out Siegel was the brains behind the NBA logo, he continued eating and acted as if Siegel wasn't there. Fast forward several years to sometime in the 2000s, and West and Siegel were reacquainted at a Lakers private club dinner. West's demeanor toward Siegel didn't change.

To this day, Siegel has no idea why West feels uncomfortable being the NBA logo. He told ANDSCAPE:

"When I did the Major League Baseball symbol, Harmon Killebrew called me and said, 'Is it based on me?' And I said, 'No, sorry.' Various people called me and said, 'Was that me? Can you say it's me?' And I said, 'No.'"

"In baseball, these guys wanted it to be them and here's West, who's the symbol of the NBA, and he's uncomfortable with it. God knows why."

Rumors of a potential change of the NBA's logo became viral in the aftermath of Lakers legend Kobe Bryant's tragic and untimely death in January 2020. NBA fans brought up the idea on Twitter to honor the late Lakers superstar. Before long, Bryant's wife Vanessa and Brooklyn Nets point guard Kyrie Irving supported the thought of Kobe becoming the new face of the NBA. Regrettably, that idea never materialized; Jerry West is still the *face of* the NBA to the present day.

Now a little more about his life on and off the court.

Jerome Alan "Jerry" West was born in Chelyan, West Virigina on May 28, 1938. West, the fifth of sixth kids, dealt with adversity at an early age. His father was so abusive, Jerry had to keep a loaded shotgun under his bed in case the latter provoked him.

Things did not get any better for West when he became an adolescent. His brother David was killed in the Korean War in 1951. Jerry was just thirteen years old when he dealt with that personal tragedy.

Jerry took out his frustrations on the basketball court. Although he was apprehensive because his scrawny frame might become susceptible to injury, he mustered enough courage and tried out for the East Bank High School basketball team. The rest is history.

West emerged from his shell and became one of the best players in West Virginia high school basketball history. He averaged a lofty thirty-two points per game and led East Bank High to the state title game in the spring of 1956. West's impressive game caught the eye of many college basketball scouts. Despite getting feelers from more than sixty college basketball programs, Jerry decided to remain in-state and commit to the West Virginia Mountaineers.

West proved he wasn't a fluke at the college level. After finishing his first year of college basketball with the freshman squad, West flourished with the varsity team under head men's basketball coach Fred Schaus. West went on to average 24.8 points per game on 50.8 percent shooting for the Mountaineers for the next three seasons. He finished his NCAA career on a strong note by averaging 29.3 points per game as a senior in the 1959-60 season.

The 6'3" West wasn't a typical shooting guard in the late 1950s. Jerry was a rebounding machine who beat taller forwards and centers for possession. West achieved the unthinkable by averaging 13.3 rebounds per game in his three seasons at West Virginia from 1957 to 1959. With West scoring at will and dominating the boards, the Mountaineers made three consecutive NCAA Tournament appearances during that same time frame. To nobody's surprise, West earned two Consensus First-Team All-American selections when he played for the Mountaineers in the late 1950s.

West became a highly-touted NBA prospect by the time he was about to turn professional in 1960. The Los Angeles Lakers made him the second overall selection of the 1960 NBA Draft. West eventually spent his entire fifteen-year NBA career with the Purple and Gold from 1960 to 1974. He averaged 27.0 points, 5.8 rebounds, and 6.7 assists during his memorable NBA career.

With West, Wilt Chamberlain, and Elgin Baylor spearheading the Lakers' attack, Los Angeles became a title contender in the 1960s and early 1970s. The Lakers won nine division titles and one NBA championship from 1960 to 1974. West earned his first and only NBA championship ring following the Lakers' record-breaking 69-13 win-loss season in 1971-72 – a record that stood for twenty-four years until Michael Jordan's Chicago Bulls won an incredible seventy-two games in the 1995-96 NBA season.

West hung up his cleats (a term for the retirement of basketball players) following the 1973-74 NBA season. He earned fourteen NBA All-Star appearances, two All-NBA Second-Team selections, and fourteen All-NBA First-Team selections in his fifteen-year NBA career. West was no slouch on defense – he earned four-time NBA All-Defensive First Team selections from 1970 to 1973.

Jerry continued piling up accolades in retirement. He is a member of the NBA's 35th-, 50th-, and 75th-anniversary teams. West is also enshrined in the Naismith Memorial Basketball Hall of Fame and the College Basketball Hall of Fame. Both the Los Angeles Lakers and West Virginia Mountaineers retired his famous No. 44 jersey.

West coached the Lakers from 1976 to 1979. He served the Lakers as a scout and general manager from 1979 to 2000. He spearheaded the drafting of highly-touted high school basketball star Kobe Bryant in 1996. Bryant went on to spend his entire twenty-year NBA career with the Lakers from 1996 to 2016.

West worked in various front-office capacities for the Memphis Grizzlies,

Golden State Warriors, and Los Angeles Clippers after he left the Lakers in 2000. He earned eight NBA championship rings as an executive – six with the Lakers (1980, 1982, 1985, 1987, and 1988) and two with the Warriors (2015 and 2017).

West, a two-time NBA Executive of the Year winner (1995 and 2004), is currently an executive board member and consultant of the Clippers.

Jerry West's incredible résumé speaks for itself; no wonder he's front and center on the NBA's logo. The league had three logos prior to its major rebranding campaign in 1969. None of the logos had the visual appeal of the current one – they featured a ball with either 'National Basketball Association' or 'NBA' at the center.

The 6'3" West's height did not make any headlines back in the day – other ballers who were much shorter or taller than him (such as Wilt Chamberlain) stood out because of their physical appearances. In the next chapter, we will discuss the controversial issue of height – does it matter in the NBA or not?

Chapter 7:
PLAYING ABOVE THE RIM: THE CONNECTION BETWEEN HEIGHT AND BASKETBALL

Did you know that the average height of players during the 2021-22 NBA season was 6'6" (198 cm) – a full eight inches taller than the average American male? Doesn't this fact make you wonder why most basketball players are so tall?

When the NBA was in its third year of existence in 1952, point guards[1] such as the Boston Celtics' Bob Cousy had an average height of 6' – the average height of today's American man.

Fast-forward some twenty-five years to the Magic Johnson era, and point guards experienced a growth spurt. Players in that position had an average height of 6'3". The 6'9" Johnson played as a point guard in the body of a power forward —a taller and stronger player who sets screens, rebounds, and scores and defends in the low post.

Magic was a rare breed who easily stood out among shorter point guards

---

1   The shortest players who handle basketball and direct the flow of the offense

of his era such as Isiah Thomas, Dennis Johnson, Gary Payton, and Terry Porter. He could easily dominate them in the low post (the shaded area near the basket) because of the height discrepancy. Although I am not a Lakers fan, I enjoyed watching Johnson run the vaunted 'Lake Show' (the term for the Lakers' fastbreak attack) during the 1980s.

Johnson was one of the few exceptions for players at his position; point guards are usually the shortest players in NBA history. Here are some of the shortest ballers the league has ever seen:

SHORTEST BALLERS

- **Mel Hirsch, 5'6**: Although Hirsch played in just fifteen games for the Boston Celtics from 1946 to 1947, he made an indelible mark on the game. He was the shortest player of the pre-NBA basketball era. In fact, Hirsch and Spud Webb were the NBA's shortest players until Tyrone "Muggsy" Bogues broke their record when he entered the pro ranks in 1987.

- **Red Klotz, 5'7"**: Klotz's name doesn't ring a bell with many basketball pundits. That's because he played in only eleven games for the Baltimore Bullets (now known as the Washington Wizards) of the defunct Basketball Association of America (BAA) in 1948. Nevertheless, Klotz earned a championship in his lone season with the Bullets that year.

- **Anthony Jerome "Spud" Webb, 5'6"**: Webb was one of the most popular short players of the 1980s. At just 5'6", Spud looked more like a college student on the basketball court. Despite his short stature, he held his own against taller point guard. Webb, who spent his first six seasons with the Atlanta Hawks, averaged 9.9 points in his twelve-year NBA career.

  Webb wasn't your typical short NBA point guard – he had an amazing forty-two-inch vertical leap. The powerful springs in Spud's legs allowed him to dunk the basketball with relative ease. When I first saw him dunk when I was in grade school, I was slack-jawed.

If you haven't watched him play, go to YouTube and watch some of his gravity-defying dunks.

The highlight of Webb's NBA career was the 1986 Slam Dunk contest in his hometown of Dallas, TX. Webb beat his teammate, 6'9" Dominique "The Human Highlight Film" Wilkins, in the final to clinch the trophy.

- **Earl Boykins, 5'5"**: When Boykins stood next to his NBA contemporaries such as 7'1" Shaquille O'Neal and 7'6" Yao Ming, he looked like a flea those two centers could easily flick with one finger. That wasn't the case, however – Boykins was stronger than many people give him credit for.

  According to SLAM, Boykins would bench press an incredible 315 pounds. Although I have been doing strength training for more than twenty years, my max bench press does not even come close to what Boykins could lift. Not only was Boykins strong, he was also durable – he played fifteen seasons in the NBA from 1998 to 2012. He averaged a decent 8.9 points per game for eleven teams during that span.

- **Tyrone "Muggsy" Bogues, 5'3"**: Bogues is the shortest player in NBA history. When Bogues stood right next to 7'7" Washington Bullets center Gheorge Muresan, they looked like the NBA's version of Mutt and Jeff.

  Bogues played in the same era as another little man, Spud Webb. Their styles of play were radically different. Webb was a high-flying point guard who could dunk in fastbreak plays. In sharp contrast, the cat-quick Bogues relied on his speed and deception to outsmart much taller players. Bogues was also an excellent passer: he averaged 10.7 assists per game twice during his fifteen-year NBA career.

On the other end of the spectrum are the tallest players in NBA history.

Although many NBA players are tall, these behemoths stood head and shoulders above everybody else during their time on the hardcourt:

TALLEST BALLERS

- **Slavko Vraneš, 7'6"**: Vranes, a Montenegro native, played on various title-winning teams in Europe. However, he was an afterthought by the time he made it to the NBA in 2004. He played in just one game, attempted one shot, and committed a personal foul in less than three minutes of playing time. Although Vranes never played in the NBA again, he is still technically one of the tallest players in NBA history.

- **Shawn Bradley, 7'6"**: Bradley was the definition of a human beanpole. His playing weight of 219 lbs. was too light for his 7'6" frame. Consequently, he looked like a stick guarding the low post for the Philadelphia 76ers, New Jersey Nets, and Dallas Mavericks during his thirteen-year NBA career. Bradley was a below-average scorer who mustered only 8.1 points per game from 1993 to 2005.

  However, scoring wasn't what Bradley's coaches wanted from him. If he could score, that was a bonus. His primary concern was defense and blocking shots. Bradley put his height to good use and blocked 2,119 shots during his NBA career.

- **Yao Ming, 7'6"**: Ming represented basketball's globalization during the early 21st century. The pride of China took the NBA by storm in 2002 and made slow, plodding centers look silly in the low post.

  Ming wasn't just tall; he was strong. Yao was almost 100 lbs. heavier than Bradley, one of his predecessors. Since Ming weighed more than 300 lbs., he could outmuscle other big men in the shaded area. Yao's battles with the Los Angeles Lakers' Shaquille O'Neal in the early 2000s were among the most memorable in NBA history.

  Ming was also the most accomplished among the tallest players in league history. He averaged 19.0 points, 9.2 rebounds, and 1.9

blocks per game from 2002 to 2011. The Houston Rockets also retired the eight-time NBA All-Star's No. 11 jersey in February 2017.

- **Manute Bol, 7'7"**: Bol, a native of Sudan, was one of the two tallest players in NBA history. Just like Bradley, Bol was a beanpole whose gangly frame made some fans think he was merely a freak of nature.

  Bol proved them wrong – he was the premier shot blocker in the NBA in the 1980s. He averaged 3.3 blocks per game in his eleven-year NBA career. Opponents had to improvise their shots in the shaded area because Bol could swat their attempts with ease. If Bol could not block the shot, his imposing height could at least alter their shots and change the dynamics of the game.

  Bol was never an offensive threat. He averaged just 2.6 points per game in his various stints with the Washington Bullets, Golden State Warriors, Philadelphia 76ers, and Miami Heat from 1985 to 1995. Although he developed a reliable three-point shot as his career progressed, he was never known for his offensive production.

  Sadly, Bol passed away due to kidney failure in the summer of 2010. His 7'2" son Bol Bol currently plays for the Orlando Magic.

- **Gheorge Muresan, 7'7"**: Muresan stood toe-to-toe with Bol in terms of height; they're the joint-tallest players in NBA history. The former played in a combined six seasons for the Washington Bullets and New Jersey Nets from 1993 to 1999.

  Muresan's best statistical season was 1995-96 when he averaged 14.5 points, 9.6 rebounds, and 2.3 blocks per game. His .584 shooting percentage also led the NBA that year. To nobody's surprise, Muresan won the 1996 NBA Most Improved Player of the Year award.

Now that we've broken down the careers of the shortest and tallest players in NBA history, the bigger question looms: Is there a connection between an NBA player's height and his productivity on the basketball court?

The website WritingBros.com conducted a recent study that answered that controversial question. The test subjects included fifty-one players from the 2018-19 NBA season. For their part, the researchers used the Pearson correlation test to determine whether the players' height had any significance on their scoring prowess. According to the researchers' website, the results showed there was no significant connection between the two variables:

"The results showed there was no significant result, a p-value of 0.197 with a statistical significance level of 0.05, so the expected hypothesis (that there is a positive correlation between the length of NBA players in the Western Conference and their average number of scores per minute played) should be rejected."

"The results of this research showed there is no relationship between length and average number of scores per minute played when taking a sample of NBA players in the Western Conference and only the data of 2018-19 is considered."

The findings seemed to make sense. If NBA fans think players should stand at least 7'5" tall so they can score at will, they're wrong. Manute Bol, a 7'6" center who played in the 1980s, averaged just 2.6 points per game in his pro basketball career. On the other hand, 5'7" Spud Webb's career scoring average of 9.9 points per game easily dwarfed Bol's. Height does not automatically translate into might, except when a big man is as talented as Yao Ming.

The clear takeaway is that an NBA player's height has nothing to do with his productivity. It's his talent level that ultimately counts in the long run.

The proof is in the pudding: although legends such as Michael Jordan, Larry Bird, and Magic Johnson were not the tallest players in NBA history, they are enshrined in the Naismith Memorial Basketball Hall of Fame in Springfield, MA. Gargantuan players such as Bol, Gheorge Muresan, and Shawn Bradley aren't.

The mistaken notion of height as an important factor of a player's productivity does not apply just to the NBA. It also applies to the Women's National Basketball Association (WNBA) – the highest level of women's basketball, which we will explore further in the next chapter.

Chapter 8:
A GAME FOR EVERYONE: THE RISE OF WOMEN'S BASKETBALL

B asketball has always revolved around skill, strategy, and teamwork. The game we love is constantly changing and evolving. In fact, women's basketball has made headlines in the past twenty-six years since the Women's National Basketball Association's (WNBA) inception in 1997.

WNBA superstars such as Tamika Catchings, Sheryl Swoopes, Cynthia Cooper, Lisa Leslie, Andrea Stinson, Marina Mabrey, Candace Parker, and Sabrina Ionescu have shown they can play at the same level as their NBA counterparts.

I can certainly attest to this. I have been following the WNBA since its inaugural season in 1997. I was a college junior that year and I enjoyed watching the league's pioneers such as Swoopes, Cooper, and Leslie strut their wares on the court.

Cooper was one of the best shooters in WNBA history. She could score forty points on any given night. Swoopes, her Houston Comets teammate, was the epitome of versatility while Leslie was a force in the low post. I also loved watching the Sacramento Monarchs' Ticha Penicheiro's fancy passing skills. She was the female version of the Sacramento Kings' Jason "White Chocolate" Williams. I still follow the WNBA with a fervent passion to this day – I am a staunch supporter of the Indiana Fever.

How did the WNBA become the premier league in women's basketball? For that, we go back in time to April 24, 1996.

The NBA's Board of Governors approved the formation of the WNBA on that day. The newfound league, whose slogan was "We Got Next," was going to kick off the following summer. Although the WNBA wasn't the first women's basketball league in the USA (that distinction belonged to the defunct WBL), it was the first the NBA supported.

The WNBA competed with the American Basketball League in the mid-1990s. Unfortunately, the latter folded during its fateful 1998-99 season. With no other leagues to compete against, the WNBA dominated the professional women's basketball landscape for the next three decades.

The WNBA had four teams each in the Eastern and Western Conferences in 1997. The Eastern Conference teams were the New York Liberty, Houston Comets, Cleveland Rockers, and Charlotte Sting. Their Western Conference counterparts were the Los Angeles Sparks, Phoenix Mercury, Utah Starzz, and Sacramento Monarchs.

The Houston Comets were the WNBA's first dynasty. With Van Chancellor calling the shots, the trio of Tina Thompson, Sheryl Swoopes, and Cynthia Cooper spearheaded a formidable Comets offense. The Comets dominated the competition and won the WNBA's first four titles from 1997 to 2000.

The WNBA expanded during Houston's four-year dynasty. The league welcomed the Detroit Shock and Washington Mystics in 1998, and the Orlando Miracle and Minnesota Lynx in 1999. The collective bargaining agreement (a contract that bound the WNBA and its players' union) in 1999 was the first in women's pro sports.

The league continued expanding in the Comets' last year of their historic four-peat. The WNBA added the Indiana Fever, Seattle Storm, Miami Sol, and Portland Fire in 2000. The addition of the four squads brought the total to sixteen as the WNBA began its fourth year of operations.

The WNBA currently has twelve teams. The Indiana Fever, Atlanta Dream, Chicago Sky, Washington Mystics, New York Liberty, and Connecticut Sun comprise the Eastern Conference. The Los Angeles Sparks, Dallas Wings, Las Vegas Aces, Seattle Storm, Phoenix Mercury, and Minnesota Lynx make up the Western Conference.

There has been a competitive balance since 2001. Although no team has established a dynasty since, several teams have won multiple championships. The most successful franchises are the Seattle Storm (four titles), Minnesota Lynx (four), Los Angeles Sparks (three), and the Detroit Shock (now known as the Dallas Wings, with three).

The development of the league has helped salaries, but not enough to compete with their NBA counterparts. In today's NBA, superstars such as the Los Angeles Lakers' LeBron James and the Golden State Warriors' Stephen Curry earn in the $30-to-$40 million range per season. This doesn't even include the millions they earn from their product endorsements and miscellaneous business endeavors.

In sharp contrast, WNBA players have earned merely a fraction of that amount over the years. Fortunately, the WNBA's collective bargaining agreement (CBA) in 2020 increased their annual pay by almost 53%. Consequently, each team's top players can earn as much as $500,000 in a season. Other talented players can earn in the $200,000-to-$300,000 range.

There's no question the WNBA has inspired young women from around the world to reach their full potential as basketball players. Ballers from Australia (Michelle Times, Lauren Jackson, Tully Bevilaqua, and Michelle Timms), Belgium (Emma Meesseman and Julie Allemand), Brazil (Janeth Arcain), Canada (Natalie Achonwa and Kia Nurse), and China (Han Xu) have made the WNBA a more competitive and global game for the past three decades and counting.

The WNBA has proven that female ballers can also compete at a high level just like their male counterparts in the NBA. The influx of superior talent over the past twenty-seven seasons has made the WNBA the gold standard of women's basketball. Below, we will delve into the careers of several WNBA legends who made an indelible mark on the pro game.

One of those legends is Sue Bird, a point guard who helped her team win three titles in three different decades. She is the only player in league history to accomplish that feat. Bird was the epitome of longevity: she played for the Storm from 2002 to 2022 and was forty-one years old when she played her final WNBA game in the 2022 WNBA season.

Bird held her jersey retirement ceremony with the Seattle Storm just one week before I started writing this chapter. The Storm hung her legendary No. 10 jersey high in the rafters of Climate Pledge Arena. She became just the second Storm player after her former teammate, Australian Lauren Jackson, to have her jersey number retired.

Indeed, Bird's career is like those of NBA basketball's Kareem Abdul-Jabbar, NFL football's Tom Brady, and even NHL hockey's Gordie "Mr. Hockey" Howe – players who defied Father Time and became one of the best their respective sports had ever produced. As for Bird, she carried the torch for women's basketball – a fire that has been lit for more than one hundred thirty years.

Women's basketball traced its humble beginnings to Smith College for Girls in Northhampton, MA, in 1892. It had been just one year since Dr. James Naismith created two makeshift basketball hoops from peach baskets at a YMCA in Springfield, MA. Physical education teacher Senda Berenson used basketball to teach her girls the finer points of teamwork and cooperation.

Berenson's rules for women's basketball were drastically different from today's game. She made them play a 'zone' type of basketball where all nine players on each team stayed within their respective areas during the game. They could only move within a five-foot radius before they passed or shot the basketball. If those rules still applied today, fans would have been bored out of their wits.

Fast forward almost forty years after Berenson formed her women's basketball teams, and professional women's basketball took the United States by storm in 1936. The All-American Redheads barnstormed[2] the country in 1936.

Team owner Oly Olsen gave them that catchy nickname to promote his wife's various salons in the Southern region. The Redheads weren't just ballers; they were also entertainers who put on a show for the crowd. They were the female counterparts of the world-famous Harlem Globetrotters.

The Redheads continued barnstorming for the next fifty years until women's college and international basketball became more popular. Those categories of women's basketball dominated ratings until the Women's National Basketball Association (WNBA) began its first year of operations in 1997.

The WNBA has produced some of the best talents the world has ever seen in its twenty-seven seasons:

Theresa Weatherspoon: She was one of the league's pioneer players and a big-time playmaker for the New York Liberty. "Spoon" was an Olympic gold medalist who helped the Louisiana Tech Lady Bulldogs win a national title during her college days. Weatherspoon and center Rebecca Lobo were the focal points of a Liberty squad that faced Cynthia Cooper's Houston Comets in three of the first WNBA Finals.

Cynthia Cooper: Cooper was one of the purest shooters in the WNBA's early years. After USC, she played for a combined ten years in Spain and Italy before joining the WNBA in 1997. She went on to become a four-time WNBA All-Star, two-time WNBA MVP, and four-time WNBA Finals MVP. Cooper, who led the league in scoring from 1997 to 1999, is also a member of the WNBA's 25th Anniversary Team.

Yolanda Griffith: Griffith was a pillar of strength for the Sacramento Monarchs in the late 1990s. She could score near the basket and knock down the mid-range jumper. A winner of both the WNBA MVP and Defensive Player of the Year in 1999, she also blocked shots, rebounded, and provided leadership on both ends of the court.

---

2   A term for travelling across the country and playing against teams from different cities and states

IN THE GAME

Diana Taurasi: She's the all-time WNBA scorer and arguably the most decorated women's player ever. A winner of three straight NCAA championships at UConn, she is a ten-time WNBA All-Star and a three-time league champion with the Phoenix Mercury. Still active following the 2023 season at age 41, Taurasi continues to play at a high level and add to her legacy.

Sue Bird: Another certain Hall of Famer with a distinguished and lengthy career, Bird retired in 2022 as one of the all-time greats. Her resume includes 13 All-Star appearances, four rings, five All-WNBA First Team selections, and five Olympic gold medals. Bird's time at UConn was capped by winning the Naismith Player of the Year and her second national championship.

Tina Thompson: Another product of the USC Lady Trojans, Thompson was an integral part of the Houston Comets' four straight titles from 1997 to 2000. The key to Thompson's success over 17 professional seasons was consistency on both ends of the floor, averaging 15.1 points and 6.2 rebounds per game. She was a nine-time WNBA All-Star and a three-time All-WNBA First Team selection.

Lauren Jackson: She's arguably the best international player in WNBA history. Jackson started playing as a four-year-old in Australia, then played for the Australian Institute of Sport and the Canberra Capitals before she became the No. 1 pick of the 2001 WNBA Draft. Like Dirk Nowitzki, a seven-footer from Germany who changed the NBA with his great shooting range, Jackson did the same for her league. She averaged nearly 19 points, and won three MVP awards and three rings.

Sheryl Swoopes: She was one of the premiere two-way players in the early years of the WNBA. Swoopes scored 15 points a game and was the one you wanted guarding the other team's best player. During her 12-year career, she was named Defensive Player of the Year three times and named to six All-Star teams. Many basketball experts compared her to the legendary Michael Jordan.

Tamika Catchings: Catchings overcame a childhood hearing impediment to become an Indiana Fever legend and a WNBA great. She was drafted out of Tennessee in 2001 and quickly made the Fever perennial title contenders.

Arguably the best defensive player in league history, Catchings was a five-time Defensive Player of the Year winner and was an All-Defensive First Team member ten times.

Lisa Leslie: Another USC great, Leslie was one of the WNBA's pioneers and became the franchise player of the Los Angeles Sparks from 1997 to 2009. She made history by becoming the first WNBA player to dunk a basketball in the summer of 2002. She was a three-time WNBA MVP, eight-time WNBA All-Star, eight-time All-WNBA First Team selection, four-time All-WNBA Second Team selection, and two-time WNBA Defensive Player of the Year.

In the next chapter, we go back to talking about one of the great men in basketball – the unstoppable Wilt Chamberlain.

Chapter 9:
THE UNSTOPPABLE WILT

You hear phrases like "larger than life," and descriptions such as "unbelievable." Often they are exaggerations. For Wilt Chamberlain, they're ideal – an unstoppable force in high school, college, and the NBA from the early 1950s through the early 1970s.

He stood 7'1", towering over opponents and blessed with an incredible physical build. He won four Most Valuable Player awards, the Rookie of the Year, two championships, a Finals MVP, and was selected to 13 All-Star Games and ten All-NBA teams. He won seven scoring titles and eleven rebounding crowns.

His statistical accomplishments include more than 70 NBA records – averaging 55 rebounds per game, 30 points and 20 rebounds in a season, 50 points and 48 minutes per contest, and 100 points in a single game.

As former teammate Billy Cunningham put it: "The NBA Guide reads like Wilt's personal diary."

Wilton Norman Chamberlain was born on August 21, 1936, in Philadelphia. He was one of many children in the household and was very shy during childhood. Being significantly taller than his classmates was, as he put it in a 1980s interview, "traumatizing." It was in sports that he truly could be himself.

Already 6'11 by the time he entered Overbrook High School, Chamberlain was a standout track and field athlete – in the high jump, long jump, shot put, and racing.

Naturally, he excelled on the court too. His remarkable size, strength, and stamina overpowered anyone in his way. During his three years at Overbrook, he scored over 2,200 points, averaging about 37 points per game, won two city championships, and earned a host of nicknames: "Wilt the Stilt," "Goliath," and "The Big Dipper."

In searching for a college, Chamberlain wanted a change of scenery. After visiting Kansas University and its legendary coach Phog Allen, Chamberlain announced he would be a Jayhawk.

Per NCAA rules at the time, Chamberlain was not allowed to play on the varsity team during his freshman year of 1955-56. But his performances on the freshman team drew large crowds and anticipation for what was to come.

In 1956-57, he averaged 29.9 points and 18.9 rebounds per game. Kansas made it all the way to the NCAA Championship Game, where they lost a triple-overtime thriller to North Carolina. Despite the defeat, Chamberlain was still named the tournament's Most Outstanding Player.

Wilt faced constant double- and triple-teaming in the title game with the Tar Heels, a defensive strategy that would continue nationwide in his junior year. Nevertheless, he averaged 30.1 points and 17.5 rebounds. His frustration with the defensive pressure on him, not to mention racial tension, was what led him to join the Harlem Globetrotters for a year before entering the NBA.

The Philadelphia Warriors selected Wilt as a territorial pick, a special draft choice that could make selections of notable local players to drive interest. Chamberlain scored 43 points and hauled in 28 rebounds in his professional debut. He won the scoring and rebounding title and his 37.6 point and 27 rebound averages each were the highest ever for a rookie. He was the first to win both Rookie of the Year and Most Valuable Player in the same season.

IN THE GAME

With each season came greater achievements – rewriting the record book with regularity. Some records are etched in stone. One such feat came on March 2, 1962 in Hershey, PA. The Warriors were facing the New York Knicks. It's a box score that defies description. He attempted 63 shots, made 36 of them, and scored a remarkable 100 points. Nobody has come close to this. Adding to the unbreakable records, during that 1961-62 campaign, Chamberlain averaged 50.4 points and 48.5 minutes a game. Regulation NBA contests only last 48 minutes, not counting overtime.

For all this, Wilt did not win MVP. Boston's Bill Russell did. Their two teams squared off for the right to make the NBA Finals. It would be the first of many postseason encounters. And it was against Russell that Chamberlain's legacy would be measured.

The Celtics prevailed in seven games, initiating a trend to follow Wilt throughout his duels with Russell. Chamberlain was the superior individual performer, but Russell was the winner. More so, Chamberlain had begun to develop a reputation: unable to succeed in big games.

In 1964, the Warriors moved to San Francisco – but Wilt wouldn't be there for long. He'd come back home in a trade to the Philadelphia 76ers.

Boston and Philadelphia met in the 1965 Eastern Conference Finals. It was another seven-game series that went the Celtics' way, with John Havlicek's dramatic steal sealing the final victory. The pattern continued throughout the decade: Wilt would compile point totals, rebounding totals that would astound and continue to prove why he was the most unstoppable offensive presence in the sport (winning multiple MVPs in the process), only to be defeated by Russell and his more dominant team.

The exception was 1966-67. In what was the greatest season ever in league history, the 76ers went 68-13 and Chamberlain repeated as MVP with 24.1 points, 24.2 rebounds, and – with an improved passing sense – 7.8 assists per game. The aging Celtics were no match for this determined Philly team. Wilt and the Sixers blew past Boston. The "Goliath" finally had a ring, after defeating the San Francisco Warriors in a six-game Finals.

He could do it all – except shoot free throws. He finished with a career foul-shooting percentage of 51.1, despite many attempts to fix his woes.

Only the Los Angeles Lakers had experienced more trouble defeating the Celtics. So in the summer of 1968, they made a trade for Wilt. Way before the days of Kevin Garnett, Ray Allen, and Paul Pierce, or LeBron James, Dwyane Wade, and Chris Bosh, this might have been the first "Big 3" in NBA history as Chamberlain joined forces with Elgin Baylor and Jerry West.

Playing alongside two other elite scorers diminished Wilt's point totals, but it was of little matter as the Lakers made it to the NBA Finals. They ran into the Celtics again, not having won in six previous meetings.

Favored Los Angeles hosted Game 7 and was poised to defeat an even more weary Boston club. But the Celtics' guile overcame the Lakers' skill. Chamberlain, dealing with a gimpy knee, begged off in the contest's critical moments – a decision that haunted him going forward. Boston won, 108-106.

Chamberlain's knee nearly derailed his 1969-70 campaign. He played in only 12 regular season games, but managed to return for the playoffs. The Lakers made it back to the Finals. But it was another injured center who took the spotlight. New York's Willis Reed overcame a bad hip to step on the floor for Game 7. Wilt was once again a non-factor as the Knicks took the title.

Redemption for him and the Lakers would come two years later. Wilt had developed a more diverse role as a passer, rebounder, defender, and scorer. Los Angeles reeled off a record 33 straight regular-season victories and a 60-22 mark. There would be no question of Chamberlain's determination, or the Lakers' ability to come through in the clutch, as Los Angeles rolled to its first-ever championship on the west coast – a five-game triumph over the Knicks.

He didn't necessarily go out a winner, but Wilt had one more season in him before hanging up the sneakers. Chamberlain left the game as the league's all-time leading scorer, which would be surpassed by Kareem Abdul-Jabbar 11 years later. The Hall of Fame induction was a foregone conclusion, made official in 1978.

IN THE GAME

Wilt made many ventures after his career. As one of the first black millionaires, he had already been highly visible. He engaged in business deals, opened a nightclub, had a stint as a professional volleyball player, and acted in movies and television shows. A 1991 autobiography revealed his infamous claim of having slept with more than 20,000 women.

Publicity and his status as a cultural icon remained for decades – up until his death in October 1999. In post-retirement, his reputation as a man who put up big stats but couldn't win the big game got larger. But in truth, with multiple rings, he might be better regarded as the most misunderstood player ever.

Misunderstood or not, Wilt Chamberlain left an indelible legacy. Though, on a global scale, there's no better place to build a legacy than at the Olympics. In our next chapter, we'll explore basketball on the world stage.

Chapter 10:
DREAMING OF GOLD: AT THE OLYMPICS

For many basketball players, representing their countries and winning the gold medal at the Olympics is the ultimate dream. But how did this sport become such a central part of the world's most prestigious athletic competition?

To answer that question, let's turn back the clock and probe deeper into the history of basketball at the Olympics. Thirteen years after Dr. James Naismith invented basketball, the game became a demonstration event at the 1904 Olympics in St. Louis, MO, USA. It wasn't until the 1936 Berlin Olympics (the same Olympics track star Jesse Owens dominated) when men's basketball became an official medal event. For its part, women's basketball became a medal event forty years later in Montreal, QC, Canada.

When players first represented the United States in men's basketball almost 90 years ago, they wore skin-tight uniforms and skimpy shorts; they barely resembled future generations of ballers who represented the Stars and Stripes.

Twenty-one teams competed for the gold medal in men's basketball in the 1936 Olympics. Even back in the day, the United States lorded it over the competition. The Americans didn't just beat their opponents; they dominated them. It became a recurring theme right up to the present day.

IN THE GAME

A prime example of Team USA's dominance in men's basketball was its 65-21 rout of France in the gold medal match at the 1948 London games. The Americans went on to beat their arch-nemesis, the Soviet Union, in the next four gold medal matches.

Despite their earlier setbacks, the Soviets remained undaunted. They rebuilt their basketball program and became a powerhouse in international competition outside of the Olympics. Their hard work paid off, as they won the European Basketball Championships ten times between the early 1950s and early 1970s. The Soviet Union eventually won the FIBA World Championships in 1972.

With that unprecedented victory, the Soviets were on a collision course with the Americans at the 1972 Olympics in Munich, Germany. Although the USA lost to the USSR in the 1970 World University Games, the former was still the favorite heading into the highly anticipated match-up two years later.

Nevertheless, the Americans lost some of their talented players to the NBA in the early '70s. Consequently, players from the college ranks represented the USA in 1972. That disadvantage gave the Soviets a valuable opportunity.

According to Olympics.com, "The Soviets had found a way to exploit the American limitation by listing their players as soldiers or workers, which allowed them to breach the amateur rules." Thus, the USSR's lineup featured experienced veterans such as Sergei Belov, Modestas Paulauskas, and Alexander Belov.

As expected, both teams breezed through the gold medal round. The Soviets' veteran savvy helped them hang tough with their American counterparts – and held a 26-21 lead at the half. Mike Bantom, a member of the American team who currently works as the NBA's senior vice president for player development, told *The New York Times* (via Olympics.org), some fifty-one years later, that the Soviets were up because they controlled the tempo.

It seemed the USSR was going to upset the USA, because they had an eight-point lead with more than six minutes left. However, the Americans made a furious comeback and trimmed the deficit to just one with six seconds remaining in regulation. USA guard Doug Collins – a future NBA star and head coach – stole the ball in the Soviets' next possession. They fouled Collins so he wouldn't score an uncontested layup.

Collins coolly sank both free throws to give the Americans a one-point lead. The USSR promptly called a timeout afterward. When the Soviets could not score in the remaining second, the Americans celebrated on the court.

However, the FIBA president asked game officials to put three seconds on the clock because of a refereeing mistake. One of the Soviet players inbounded the ball from the opposite end of the court and threw a desperation pass to center Alexander Belov.

Belov miraculously caught the desperation heave and scored on an uncontested layup as time expired. The USSR stunned the USA, 51-50. It was the latter's first loss in sixty-four games in Olympic competition. The Americans were so furious, they refused to accept their silver medals – they became the first team in any Olympic sport to take that action.

Despite the heartbreaking loss, the Americans bounced back and won the gold medal in 1976. The then-Yugoslavian squad won gold in 1980 while the USA earned the gold medal in the 1984 Los Angeles Olympics. That 1984 team featured future NBA stars Michael Jordan, Chris Mullin, Patrick Ewing, Alvin Robertson, Sam Perkins, Steve Alford, and Wayman Tisdale. Their coach was legendary Indiana Hoosiers head man Bobby Knight.

After the Soviet Union won their final gold medal in men's basketball in the 1988 Seoul Olympics, the USA has dominated the sport to the present day. The turning point came during the 1992 Barcelona Olympics, when FIBA, the international governing body of basketball, allowed professionals to play for their respective national teams.

The Americans pounced on the opportunity. They assembled what was arguably the greatest team in sports history – 'The Dream Team.' Team USA featured Michael Jordan, Larry Bird, Magic Johnson, Scottie Pippen, Patrick Ewing, Clyde Drexler, David Robinson, Karl Malone, Charles Barkley, Chris

Mullin, and John Stockton. Duke Blue Devils forward Christian Laettner was the only college player on the roster.

'The Dream Team' routed its first seven opponents in convincing fashion. The Americans throttled Croatia in the gold medal game, 117-85. They made a resounding statement that they were the best in the world in men's basketball. That trend has continued. Team USA has won six of the past seven gold medals in their Olympic event. They won bronze in the 2004 Athens Olympics, their worst finish in sixteen years.

Team USA has also been the gold standard in women's basketball since its inception in the 1976 Montreal Olympics. After the Soviets won the first two gold medals in 1976 and 1980, the Americans have won nine of the past ten gold medals in women's basketball.

Olympic basketball has evolved in the last several years. The International Olympic Committee's (IOC) executive board announced in the summer of 2017 that 3x3 basketball would become an official Olympic event in Tokyo three years later. Since the COVID-19 pandemic broke out in 2020, the IOC postponed the games until the following year.

Eight teams (Latvia, Belgium, China, Japan, Netherlands, Poland, Russia, and Serbia) competed in the men's 3x3 basketball event. The Latvians beat the Russians in the gold medal game, 21-18. Eight teams participated in women's 3x3 basketball: China, Japan, France, Italy, Mongolia, Russia, Romania, and the United States. The Americans prevailed over the Russians in the gold medal game, 18-15.

There have been many memorable moments in Olympic basketball since its debut in Berlin, Germany in 1936. Here are ten of these unforgettable moments:

1. **USSR beats the USA in the gold medal game, 1972 Munich Olympics**: It wasn't just an exciting finish – it was one of the most controversial games in Olympic history. When the officials added three seconds to regulation time, it changed the complexion of the game. Alexander Belov's buzzer-beating layup gave the Soviets a pulsating 51-50 win.

2. **Soviets defeat the Americans in the semifinals, 1988 Seoul Olympics**: It was bound to happen – the USA and USSR were on a collision course for Olympic gold in Seoul, South Korea in 1988. Their controversial gold medal game sixteen years earlier set the stage for another scintillating rematch the world wanted to watch. In the bigger scheme of things, the rematch took place during the latter part of the Cold War between the two superpowers. This time around, the Soviets – who had NBA stars Arvydas Sabonis and Sarunas Marciulionis – won convincingly, 92-76.

3. **'The Dream Team' annihilates the competition, 1992 Barcelona Olympics**: The United States made a resounding statement several weeks after FIBA announced that professional players could represent their respective countries. The moment 'The Dream Team,' consisting of Michael Jordan, Larry Bird, Magic Johnson, Scottie Pippen, Clyde Drexler, David Robinson, Patrick Ewing, Karl Malone, and Charles Barkley was assembled, it was blatantly obvious nobody was going to beat them. True enough, the Americans reclaimed their rightful place as the best in men's basketball in the Olympics.

4. **Women's Team USA wins gold, 1996 Atlanta Olympics**: What could be sweeter than winning the gold medal on your home soil in front of your countrymen? That's how Team USA's women's basketball team – a group led by Lisa Leslie, Sheryll Swoopes, and Dawn Staley – felt when they crushed Brazil 111-87 in the gold medal game and punctuated an undefeated 8-0 stint at the Olympics.

5. **Vince Carter dunks over Frederic Weis, 2000 Sydney Olympics**: Ballers such as LeBron James, Steph Curry, Russell Westbrook, Kawhi Leonard, and Anthony Davis make headlines nowadays. It's just a shame many basketball fans don't pay tribute to Vince Carter.

   The man known as "Vinsanity" was one of the best dunkers of the late 1990s and early 2000s NBA. Carter, who represented Team USA in the 2000 Sydney Olympics, showed everyone why he was the 2000 NBA slam dunk champion in a game against France. After

Team USA's Gary Payton missed a layup, the French grabbed the rebound. Carter stole the outlet pass and had only one thing in mind – to dunk the ball with authority.

As Carter drove to the basket, French center Frederic Weis stood in his way so he could take a charge (a basketball term for an offensive foul or a foul on a player with the ball when he plows into a defensive player). Carter improvised, leapt over the 7'2" Weis, and threw down a vicious tomahawk dunk.

Carter screamed his lungs out and pumped his fist afterward (I saw the dunk in real time and couldn't believe what I just saw. If you haven't seen it yet, go to YouTube and search up 'Vince Carter Olympic dunk'). As for Weis, he has remained Carter's poster boy for the past twenty-three years.

6. **Argentina upsets Team USA, 2004 Athens Olympics**: With the embarrassing losses to Puerto Rico and Lithuania behind them, Team USA wanted to gain traction and outright entry into the gold medal match with a win over Argentina in the semifinal round. Unfortunately for the Americans, the Argentinians had other ideas. The latter's core group included NBA stars Manu Ginobili, Andres Nocioni, and Luis Scola. Argentina held the USA to 41.6 percent shooting for the field and held on for a crucial 89-81 win. The loss relegated Team USA to the bronze medal game.

7. **Puerto Rico upsets Team USA, 2004 Athens Olympics**: 'Dream Team III' failed to live up to the massive hype in Athens Greece in 2004. A core group that included LeBron James, Carmelo Anthony, Dwyane Wade, Allen Iverson, Tim Duncan, and Lamar Odom seemed unbeatable on paper. Unfortunately, the law of averages caught up with the Americans when the Puerto Ricans upset them in convincing fashion in the first game of the tournament, 92-73. Not only did the loss snap Team USA's twenty-four-game winning streak at the Olympics, but it also was their biggest loss on that stage to date.

8. **'The Redeem Team' earns gold, 2008 Beijing Olympics**: The so-called 'Redeem Team' was aptly named, sixteen years after their NBA predecessors blew out the competition in Barcelona. NBA ballers such as Kobe Bryant, LeBron James, Carmelo Anthony, Chris Paul, Dwight Howard, and Jason Kidd were set on making up for Team USA's downright embarrassing bronze medal finish in Athens four years earlier. This group made good on its promise and beat Spain 118-107 in the gold medal game.

9. **Kobe Bryant's second-half performance against Spain, 2008 Beijing Olympics**: Los Angeles Lakers legend Kobe Bryant proved he could excel on the Olympic stage during the 2008 Beijing Olympics.

    Team USA was recovering from an embarrassing bronze medal finish in the 2004 Athens Olympics four years earlier. 'The Redeem Team' was out for redemption. Bryant led the charge for the Americans in Beijing.

    With Team USA leading Spain 91-89 in the fourth quarter of the gold medal game, Bryant scored thirteen of his twenty points in the fourth quarter. Not only that, but he also had two timely assists to Deron Williams and Tim Duncan during a key fourth-quarter spurt that helped the Americans win the gold medal, 118-107.

10. **Liz Cambage becomes first female athlete to dunk in Olympic competition, 2012 London Olympics**: Australia's Liz Cambage showed everybody that women can also defy gravity in Olympic basketball competition.

    Cambage made history by becoming the first women's basketball player to dunk in the Olympics. Her milestone occurred during a game against Russia in the 2012 London Olympics. The 6'8" Cambage received a pass at the top of the key (the farthest distance of the three-point line facing the basket), saw an open lane, dribbled once, and dunked the ball with her right hand. It was truly a memorable moment for Olympic basketball fans everywhere.

Olympic basketball has made a profound impact on the world. It's clear the United States has become the gold standard for this competition. Team USA's dominance has motivated other countries to improve their respective basketball programs over the years – they want to dethrone the Americans from the world stage. Among the most competitive basketball programs are Spain, Argentina, Brazil, China, Turkey, Canada, and Russia.

Not only that, but the Olympic games have also influenced how professional basketball players conduct business. For instance, many ballers refuse to play in the Olympics because an injury could jeopardize their chances of landing a hefty paycheck in the National Basketball Association (NBA).

However, Australian point guard Patty Mills, who plays for the NBA's Brooklyn Nets, was one of the exceptions. He told *The Associated Press* in 2021 his commitment to his national team takes precedence over his NBA career.

"This is a lifetime of work in a matter of couple of weeks," Mills said in the days leading up to the opening of the 2020 Tokyo Olympics. "I'm making sure there are no distractions for me or my teammates."

French forward Nicolas Batum also shared the same sentiment, according to *The Associated Press*. Batum, who signed a five-year, $120 million deal with the Charlotte Hornets in 2016, currently plays for the Los Angeles Clippers.

Since professional players represent their countries in the Olympics, their paychecks have become bigger in recent years. For instance, Team USA's combined NBA payroll and endorsement earnings during the 2016 Rio de Janeiro Olympics was a staggering $257 million, *Forbes* reported.

Basketball has become one of the most anticipated events of the Olympics. Since it made its debut at the 1936 Berlin Olympics, we have seen many milestones such as the Soviets' stunning victory over the USA in 1972, Vince Carter's dunk over Frederic Weis in 2000, and Team USA's first gold medal in women's basketball in 1996.

Now that we've looked at some of the broader strokes of international basketball competitions, let's dive a little deeper and look at a player who was part of one of the above-mentioned upsets, but who otherwise had an incredible career: Allen Iverson.

Chapter 11:
THE ANSWER: ALLEN IVERSON

There are few players who come into the league and display a type of ability the game hasn't seen before. Allen Iverson, however, is a definite 'one of one' athlete.

He is a player who can't be defined by statistics. You had to watch him on the court.

Small? Certainly. Tough? No question. A warrior by basketball standards.

Appreciation for the man nicknamed "The Answer" or "A.I.", has surfaced from the recent generation of players who looked up to Iverson for carrying himself unapologetically.

He did not conform to what the public wanted him to look like. He didn't shy away from driving in the lane with his undersized frame and taking on taller, bigger players waiting to rough him up by the basket. Iverson took all the physical punishment and thrived.

For fourteen seasons, he averaged 41.1 minutes and 26.7 points per game. He was the league scoring champion four times, including 2001 – the year he won the league's Most Valuable Player award.

It was also in that 2000-01 season in which he was the driving force behind the Philadelphia 76ers reaching their first NBA Finals in nearly two decades.

IN THE GAME

Although the Sixers lost to the Los Angeles Lakers dynasty, this was a tremendous personal achievement considering what Iverson endured in the years prior to being a prominent national basketball talent.

While still a high schooler in 1993, Iverson and a group of friends were involved in a brawl at a bowling alley in Hampton, Virginia. During the altercation, Iverson allegedly struck a woman with a chair.

He was arrested and charged with multiple offenses, including a felony for maiming by mob. Tried as an adult, Iverson was sentenced to fifteen years in prison – a decision that many felt was a clear instance of him being targeted because of his race and athletic ability.

Iverson served about four months in prison before the conviction was overturned in 1995, at which point he was released.

With a new perspective, and motivation beyond comprehension, Iverson attended Georgetown University under its legendary head coach John Thompson.

His ability showed through right away as a freshman. His speed, agility, scoring prowess, and defensive mindset helped him claim Big East Rookie of the Year.

Despite the controversy, Iverson continued to excel at Georgetown. In his sophomore year, he led the team in scoring and steals, averaging 25 points per game. His exceptional performance earned him the Big East Defensive Player of the Year award and a selection to the All-Big East First Team.

Iverson played one more season at Georgetown, leading the Hoyas as far as the Elite 8 of the NCAA Men's Basketball Tournament. Everyone knew, himself included, that he was ready to turn pro.

The Philadelphia 76ers made Iverson the No. 1 overall pick in the 1996 NBA Draft. From the start, he was a draw. An iconic moment of his initial season came on March 12, 1997, against the perennial champion Chicago Bulls. Iverson was handling the ball above the three-point line, facing the basket. Facing him was Michael Jordan. Iverson dribbled to his left, then his right, then his left, then his right – a set of crossover moves that fooled the GOAT

– before hitting a jump shot.

Iverson finished 1996-97 as the NBA Rookie of the Year, averaging 23.5 points, 7.5 assists, and 4.1 rebounds per game. His confidence was already apparent, and it grew in the ensuing years.

That was especially true in 2000-01. By then, he already had a scoring title and was fourth in the race for MVP two years before. Now he was set to lead a team further in the postseason than the franchise had been in quite a while.

Iverson claimed a second scoring crown, averaging more than 31 points a contest. He led the league in steals per game. He played 42 minutes per game. And the Sixers had the best record in the Eastern Conference. Philly took care of Indiana, fought its way through Toronto, and battled past Milwaukee to reach the NBA Finals.

Iverson's productivity increased in the postseason. He had a 32.9 point average and rarely spent a minute on the bench.

His defining moment of this playoff run, and maybe of his career, came in the series Philadelphia lost. It was hard for anyone, even Iverson, to conceive of beating the Lakers superteam of Shaquille O'Neal and Kobe Bryant. But Iverson never lacked confidence. It was ever-present in Game 1. The Sixer guard faked his defender, Tyronne Lue, to the ground and hit a crucial shot in overtime – then stepped over him. It was the only game Philly won.

Over the course of his entire career, Iverson was misunderstood – because of the way he looked, because of his on-court attitude, and because his statistics showed an overabundance of shot-taking.

This misconception was apparent in another iconic moment of his career. In a press conference on May 7, 2002, Iverson addressed questions about his practice habits with the team. Iverson mentioned "practice" repeatedly, stressing the irrelevance of the reporters' focus on something other than his performance in actual games, and the theme of his rant has stayed with him to this day. It's a culturally known sound bite, and a moment which displayed his rare emotional frankness.

IN THE GAME

While modern analytics haven't been kind to Iverson, many who followed have. The appreciation has poured in recently – both from players who idolize him and from the team with which he'll always be associated.

The 76ers traded Iverson to the Denver Nuggets on December 19, 2006, marking the end of Iverson's storied tenure with Philadelphia. He was thirty-one, but an old thirty-one. The years of fearlessness were taking their toll.

Iverson would be an All-Star four more times. He never scored with the regularity he did in Philly. After a season-and-a-half in Denver, the Nuggets traded him to the Detroit Pistons. That stay was even more brief. He was dealt to the Memphis Grizzlies in 2009, his tenure there proving shorter still: he played just three games with Memphis.

Iverson's last NBA stop was the same as his first. He returned to the 76ers for the 2009-10 season, signing a one-year contract. After one season playing with clearly diminished skills, his career came to an end. He had brief stints playing internationally, including in Turkey, before officially calling it quits from professional basketball in 2013. He was inducted into the Hall of Fame three years later.

Iverson's departure from basketball marked the end of an era – a passing of the torch by one of the sport's most unique figures.

Iverson and many others owe a debt to the game's pioneers, and a style of play that allowed for creativity and expression.

In the next chapter, lets take a look at some of the greatest black athletes in basketball.

Make a Difference with Your Review

In the Game

"Teamwork makes the dream work." – John C. Maxwell

People who give without expecting anything in return live longer, happier lives. So if we've got a chance to do that during our time together, let's make it happen.

To make that happen, I have a question for you...

Would you help someone you've never met, even if you never got credit for it?

My mission is to make basketball stories and facts accessible to everyone. Everything I do stems from that mission. And, the only way for me to accomplish that mission is by reaching...well...everyone.

This is where you come in. Most people do, in fact, judge a book by its cover (and its reviews). So here's my ask on behalf of a basketball fan you've never met:

Please help that basketball fan by leaving this book a review.

Your gift costs no money and less than 60 seconds to make real, but can change a fellow reader's life forever. Your review could help...

- One more young player find the courage to chase their basketball dreams.
- One more coach find new strategies to inspire their team.
- One more fan discover the joy of the game.
- One more aspiring athlete learn from the pros.
- One more basketball dream come true.

To get that 'feel good' feeling and help this person for real, all you have to do is...and it takes less than 60 seconds... leave a review.

Scan the QR code below to leave your review on Amazon (just so you know, this takes you to the review page of Amazon US, if you live in a different country, simply change the .com to the relevant country domain

IN THE GAME

suffix. Or you can go to your order page to leave a review there):

If you feel good about helping a faceless basketball fan, you are my kind of person. Welcome to the club. You're one of us.

I'm that much more excited to help share more basketball facts with you. You'll love the stories and lessons I'm about to share in the coming chapters.

Thank you from the bottom of my heart. Now, back to our regularly scheduled program.

Your biggest fan, Jamie Adler

PS - Fun fact: If you provide something of value to another person, it makes you more valuable to them. If you'd like goodwill straight from another basketball fan - and you believe this book will help them - send this book their way.

Chapter 12:
THE SECRET GAME

Black athletes have dominated basketball in the recent past. According to racial equality activist Richard Lapchick, black athletes comprised 73.2% of the NBA's players in 2021. The other races trailed them considerably: that year, the NBA's other racial demographics were just 16.85% white, 3.1% Latino, and 0.4% Asian.

Remarkably, the NBA's racial integration began just one year after its inaugural season in 1949. Three African-American men were the pioneers of that breakthrough, according to NBA.com's Steve Aschburner:

Chuck Cooper, Boston Celtics: Cooper was the first African-American player who entered the NBA ranks via the draft. The Celtics drafted him thirteenth overall on April 25, 1950. An owner of another NBA team told Celtics owner Walter Brown that Cooper was a "colored" player. Brown told him in no uncertain terms he didn't care about his skin color – all he cared about was his potential to help the Celtics become title contenders.

Nat "Sweetwater" Clifton, New York Knicks: Basketball historians say Clifton was the first African-American player to sign an NBA contract. He left the Harlem Globetrotters and signed with the New York Knicks just one month after the Celtics drafted Chuck Cooper.

Earl Lloyd, Washington Capitols: The Capitols drafted Lloyd 100th overall in

1950. He became the first African-American player to see action in an NBA game. Lloyd made history when he played against the Rochester Royals (now known as the Sacramento Kings) on October 31, 1950. Lloyd made NBA history again five years after the Capitols drafted him – he and his Syracuse Nationals teammate Jim Tucker became the first African-American teammates to win the league title, in 1955.

Cooper, Clifton, and Lloyd gave credit to Brooklyn Dodgers second baseman Jackie Robinson for breaking racial barriers in the NBA. Robinson became the first African-American player to take the field in Major League Baseball on April 15, 1947. It had only been three years since Robinson broke the color barrier in the majors when Cooper, Clifton, and Lloyd followed suit in professional basketball.

"Mr. Lloyd, and my dad, too, gave Jackie a lot of credit for making things easier for them," Cooper's son, Chuck III, told Aschburner in March 2022.

According to Chuck III, Robinson didn't get much support when he entered the pro baseball ranks in 1947. In sharp contrast, his dad had a support system that included Brown, head coach Red Auerbach and his teammates Bob Cousy and Bill Sharman. Cooper hit it off with Cousy and Sharman – they remained good friends for many years after they retired from professional basketball.

The younger Cooper also told NBA.com that his dad, Clifton, and Lloyd looked out for each other during their time in the NBA – a time when racial tensions ran high in the United States. The three black NBA players had a pact: they would look out for and protect each other at all costs.

For instance, whenever the Celtics played on the road in Washington, Cooper would look out for Lloyd. The latter, in turn, would return the favor when he and his teammates played in Boston. This pattern repeated frequently, since there weren't many NBA teams in the early 1950s.

Cooper, Clifton, and Lloyd are enshrined in the Naismith Memorial Basketball Hall of Fame in Springfield, MA, but — despite their camaraderie and eventual success — the three NBA African-American pioneers also had their share of tough times during the early 1950s. Many hotels refused to admit them, and many restaurants also denied them meals whenever they ate out. Cousy, one of the greatest point guards in NBA history, volunteered to ride with Cooper on a late-night train to another destination when the Celtics' hotel refused to let Cooper check in.

More African-Americans entered the NBA ranks in the next several decades. In fact, there has been a massive paradigm shift in terms of NBA demographics: black players have dominated the NBA landscape from the 1980s to the present day.

Why are there more black players than white players in the National Basketball Association? Historically black colleges and universities (HBCUs) have played a major role in this paradigm shift. These schools gave African-American players valuable opportunities to improve their skills during their college days. Later, basketball scouts visited their campuses, drafted them, and eventually signed them to lucrative NBA contracts.

Many of these HBCU players entered the NBA between the early 1960s and early 1980s. The influx of these black athletes dramatically shifted the NBA's demographics in their favor.

Another influence on the league has been streetball, which is predicated on creativity and improvisation. Many legends of the NBA have honed their skills on the streets and brought this style of play to the professional level. Streetball emphasizes one-on-one play and individual skill development. Players who excel in this format often possess exceptional ball-handling, shooting, and defensive abilities.

Beyond what skills this style brings, it also provides massive entertainment value. The NBA has incorporated elements of streetball which showcase players' individual styles and personalities into its marketing and gameplay to enhance the fan enjoyment.

The mecca for streetball is Rucker Park, located in the Harlem neighborhood of New York City. It's been a spot where many legends have been made dating back to the 1950s, and has served as a proving ground for aspiring basketball players looking to make a name for themselves.

Julius Erving, Kareem Abdul-Jabbar, Earl "The Pearl" Monroe, Kobe Bryant,

IN THE GAME

Kevin Durant, and LeBron James have all played there. The games are also legendary – with match-ups featuring the icons of streetball. Featuring passionate and enthusiastic crowds, Rucker Park is a gathering place for the community and brings people together to celebrate the sport.

Rucker Park's legacy extends beyond setting. It has shaped streetball culture and its iconic status has inspired countless other streetball courts and tournaments – in the United States and internationally.

Streetball is now played all over the world, and its influence can be seen in the playing styles of international NBA players. Players from countries like Serbia, Argentina, and Lithuania bring unique skills and techniques influenced by their experiences playing streetball in their home countries. This globalization of basketball has enriched the NBA with diverse playing styles and cultural influences.

While the sport has no doubt been enhanced by this style over the course of decades, that doesn't mean it has been smooth sailing the entire time. After a lull which threatened to see the league fade into obscurity, the NBA was revived in the 1980s thanks primarily to two players who go by singular names: Bird and Magic.

Chapter 13:
BIRD, MAGIC, AND THE '80S REVIVAL

It was critical casting. The NBA's two most storied franchises obtaining the two most promising college standouts, each with opposite backgrounds but with similar mindsets.

In 1979, Larry Bird, from French Lick, Indiana joined the Boston Celtics and Magic Johnson, from Lansing, Michigan, was drafted first overall by the Los Angeles Lakers. Together, they were the leading characters in reviving the NBA.

Before their arrival, the league was at best fledgling, and at worst on the verge of extinction. Drug problems were rampant. Attendance was down. The NBA Finals were broadcast on tape delay, airing long after they had ended so that the networks could maintain higher ratings with more popular prime-time programming.

But there was a ray of hope as early as the '79 NCAA Tournament, when their respective schools met for the national championship. Bird's Indiana State University was unbeaten heading into the title game versus Johnson's Michigan State University. Their presence lifted college basketball.

That title game, won by Magic and the Spartans, became one of the most remembered Finals in history. It's still the highest-rated NCAA game ever, and a contest that captivated the country. More importantly, it showed that college basketball can produce stars who are able to transcend the schools they represent.

The Bird-Magic showdown in Salt Lake City was a turning point for the tournament, which soon became one of sport's most lucrative properties.

The success these two provided college basketball, however, paled in comparison to the exponential growth in popularity they brought to the NBA after going pro. It's easy to see why: they rekindled the NBA's most significant rivalry, and created the best personal duel the sport has ever seen.

Bird was a fair-haired white shooter from the sticks of Indiana. His blue-collar personality meshed perfectly with Boston's blue-collar attitude. Magic Johnson was a black 6'9" point guard from Urban, Michigan – a 1,000-watt smile, gregarious, with flair on the court ideal for Hollywood. Both had upper-echelon basketball IQs, with unmatched floor vision and passing abilities. The teams, in turn, mirrored the personalities of their star players. The Celtics played hard-nosed. The Lakers were up-tempo 'Showtime.'

Their impact was immediate. Bird won the 1979-80 NBA Rookie of the Year, while Magic was the NBA Finals MVP. He filled in for an injured Kareem Abdul-Jabbar in Game 6 at Philadelphia, played all five positions and scored 42 points as Los Angeles won the franchise's seventh NBA championship.

Boston returned to prominence the very next year, with Bird leading the way, and anticipation grew on the prospect of another Celtics-Lakers rematch in the near future. The fans got their wish by 1984.

Facing off three times during the decade, the two teams added to their storied legacies while the main characters rose to even greater stature.

Each series had their own dramatic tale. The 1984 Finals went the distance, with the Celtics prevailing in a dramatic seventh game at Boston Garden. They met the next year and the Lakers – at long last – triumphed over Boston, after nine tries.

Two years later, they locked horns once more. Game 4 of the '87 Finals in Boston, with the Lakers up two-games-to-one, is arguably the defining moment for Bird-Magic. A 16-point Celtic lead was erased, the Lakers went ahead, then Larry Legend drilled a go-ahead three in the final minute. Los Angeles answered with Johnson connecting on a 'Baby Hook' in the lane. Bird's last-ditch shot was off, and the Lakers were on their way to the title.

In every year of the decade, at least Larry Bird or Magic Johnson's teams were represented in the NBA Finals.

Bird won three titles – '81, '84, and again in 1986 as the Celtics produced one of the greatest teams in history. He claimed three league MVPs as well as twelve All-Star appearances and nine All-NBA First-Team selections in his thirteen seasons. Magic won five titles – '80, another in '82 over the Philadelphia 76ers, '85, '87, and in '88 the Lakers became the first team since Bill Russell's Celtics to go back-to-back, when they defeated the Detroit Pistons in seven games. Like Bird, Johnson also won three MVPs, made twelve All-Star teams and was chosen for the All-NBA First-Team nine times.

Their close competition created a unique bond which has lasted beyond their careers. It's the friendliest, fiercest rivalry sports has ever known. It allowed the NBA to become a form of entertainment. The media embraced the rivalry, and the pair seemed to flourish in it as well. They were loyal to their cities and their organizations, and that faithfulness played well to fans everywhere.

While Bird retired mainly due to back injuries after the 1991-92 season, Magic Johnson left the game abruptly in November 1991 after stunning the nation with the announcement that he had HIV. Johnson has since been able to combat the virus, and even made brief comebacks.

There were many other superstars and super teams in the '80s. Michael Jordan emerged as one such star after joining the league in 1984, and became the must-watch player in the game. Julius Erving was certainly a predecessor to Jordan in terms of showmanship. He retired in 1987 as one of the most respected men to lace up the sneakers, and the godfather of highlight reel plays. His arrival to the league came after laboring in relative obscurity as the best player in the American Basketball Association (ABA), which folded in 1976.

Erving's search for an NBA crown was realized in 1983, as his Philadelphia 76ers were the dominant force. They had acquired Moses Malone at center, and were nearly unstoppable both in the regular season and throughout the playoffs. Losing just once in their run to the title, the Sixers swept the Lakers.

As the decade progressed, the Detroit Pistons became the biggest challengers to the Celtics' and Lakers' stranglehold on championships. They were known as the "Bad Boys" for their physical style of play and were led by Isiah Thomas, Joe Dumars, and Dennis Rodman.

After nearly missing out on the '88 title, Detroit came back with a vengeance in 1989. The Pistons swept the Lakers in the Finals on their way to consecutive championships.

The league went prime time across the United States, and the benefit was the opportunity to expand. The NBA added four new teams during the 1980s: the Miami Heat, the Charlotte Hornets, the Minnesota Timberwolves, and the Orlando Magic.

Expansion wasn't limited to the United States. The game gained plenty of international popularity, thanks in part to players like Hakeem Olajuwon (Nigeria), Dražen Petrovi· (Croatia), and Vlade Divac (Serbia). They helped the growing global talent pool, and paved the way for future superstars like Dirk Nowitzki, Luca Don·i·, and Nikola Joki·.

The 1980s were a transformative period for the NBA, setting the stage for its continued growth under Michael Jordan — who ignited fans just as Magic and Bird had — and popularity in the years to come.

While the players are vital to the sport's well-being, let's see how jerseys themselves have undergone a significant revolution through the years.

Chapter 14:
JERSEY STORY

Have you ever wondered why the previous basketball uniforms were so different than what we see now in the NBA?

If you haven't seen the jerseys the NBA's forefathers such as George Mikan, Vern Mikkelsen, Bill Russell, and Bob Cousy wore, you're in for a shock. Try looking up their old school uniforms on Google Images and you'll see skin-tight shorts and jerseys that seemed to latch onto their skins. I can't help but wonder: How were they able to breathe and play to the best of their abilities?

Their predecessors hardly resembled future NBA ballers – they wore knee-length padded pants that made them look more like football players than their basketball counterparts. Basketball players in the 1920s and 1930s ditched the pants in favor of medium-length shorts.

If you lived in the 1950s, you'd see NBA players wearing the basics: numbers, letters, and plain jerseys minus their team colors. According to the NBA's official website, those players wore shorts that were just three inches long at the inseams. One constant that has defied Father Time is the way NBA players tuck their jerseys into their shorts – you'll never see these ballers tuck their shirts out whenever they're playing. Otherwise, officials will stop play and ask the offending player to tuck in his jersey.

Players also wore socks that almost reached their knees in the 1950s and 1960s. It wasn't merely the prevailing look of those decades – knee-high socks helped protect the players' legs from excessive contact.

In terms of shoes, the majority of NBA players during Bill Russell's and Wilt Chamberlain's era wore Converse Chuck Taylors. Although those shoes looked casual by today's standards, they were the prevailing trend during the NBA's first two decades. I thought the way they ran up and down the court was remarkable – I feel 'Chucks' (the shoes' nickname) didn't have much traction, so slipping was inevitable. Fortunately, the NBA's pioneers found a way to make it work.

While short trousers, skin-tight jerseys, and 'Chucks' were the norm back in the day, there were a few trendsetters in the old NBA. Two legends quickly come to mind: Wilt "The Stilt" Chamberlain and "Pistol" Pete Maravich.

The 7'1", 275-lb. Chamberlain also earned the nickname "The Big Dipper" because he played much bigger than his opponents. Bear in mind Chamberlain set the NBA record with 100 points in a single game against the New York Knicks on March 2, 1962. Only the late Kobe Bryant came close to matching that total with his insane eighty-one-point outburst against the Toronto Raptors forty-four years later.

Why was Chamberlain a trendsetter? Simple – he was one of the first NBA players who wore headbands. He didn't wear the accessory during his first few years in the NBA. However, he began wearing it in the late 1960s when he played for the Los Angeles Lakers. When you watch old, grainy footage of the NBA of that era, you'll notice Chamberlain was the only guy who wore a headband – a trend that has become popular in today's NBA.

As Chamberlain reached the twilight of his professional basketball career, younger guys such as LSU Tigers scoring champion "Pistol" Pete Maravich entered the NBA ranks. Maravich was a skinny 6'5" point guard who mesmerized fans with his high-wire acts, trick shots, and fancy passes. They had never seen somebody with that kind of basketball arsenal in the past.

Maravich was the only one who could hang in the air and score with ease, even with two or three defenders draped all over him. The "Pistol" also had exceptional court vision: he could pass the ball to a teammate while he was looking the other way. Moves like that befuddled the opposition, to say the least. Maravich's antics paved the way for exciting point guards such as the Sacramento Kings' Jason "White Chocolate" Williams many decades later. I feel it's a shame many of today's NBA fans have no idea who the great "Pistol" Pete Maravich was.

It wasn't just Maravich's moves that made him a special player; he had a unique look that made him stand out from his contemporaries. Maravich's floppy hair, skin-tight jersey and shorts, and floppy socks were his trademark look. "Pistol" Pete's floppy socks were a clear indication that more NBA players were drifting away from the once-popular high-sock look.

The short trousers remained the NBA's prevalent look during the first few years of Larry Bird's and Magic Johnson's careers in the early 1980s. That trend changed when Chicago Bulls rookie Michael Jordan requested longer shorts in 1984. Although Jordan was just a first-year player, he had tremendous marketing appeal dating back to his college days at North Carolina. Before long, Jordan's contemporaries did away with the short trousers and started wearing longer shorts.

Hip-hop culture permeated the National Basketball Association in the 1990s. Big-name stars such as Shaquille O'Neal, Allen Iverson, and many of their fellow African-American players were at the forefront of his paradigm shift. Shorts weren't just long – they became so baggy, some of them looked like warm-up pants (the pants players wear while they are taking warm-up shots prior to the game).

As the NBA ushered in the twenty-first century, ballers began using various accessories that gave them a unique look and helped them play better. The headband Wilt Chamberlain first wore with the Los Angeles Lakers has become a common accessory in today's NBA – Jimmy Butler, Anthony Davis, Klay Thompson, Andrew Nembhard, and Myles Turner all wear headbands. Knee braces and wristbands are other common accessories players have worn since the 1970s.

One accessory that has taken the league by storm is the armband. As the name implies, it's a band that covers up a large area of a player's arm (the only area that's exposed is the player's shoulder/rotator cuff area). Players wear armbands to keep their muscles warm. This, in turn, helps ward off injury and soreness. Some players also wear arm bands to conceal their tattoos. Philadelphia 76ers point guard Allen Iverson made arm bands popular in the late 1990s and early 2000s. Other popular players such as the Denver Nuggets' Carmelo Anthony followed suit.

Many of today's NBA players also wear mouthguards for obvious reasons. Although this accessory seems more fitting for boxers, MMA fighters, and hockey players, ballers need them because basketball is a contact sport. You never know when another player's flailing elbows strike you flush in the mouth and knock several of your teeth loose. For that reason, wearing mouthguards has become a necessity in the modern NBA.

On the other hand, fans have proudly worn and flaunted their favorite NBA team's and players' jerseys since the 1980s. Whether you watch a game at an arena or a sports bar, do the groceries, or jog at the local park, there's a great chance you will see NBA fans wear their favorite jerseys like a badge of honor.

One of the biggest and most controversial jersey modifications is the sleeved jersey – a team uniform that covers a player's sleeves and most of his upper arms. The front of the sleeved jersey shows the player's number and team name while the back shows the player's number and last name.

Adidas introduced the modification in December 2013, to the dismay of many NBA players, who didn't like the new look. Cleveland Cavaliers forward LeBron James even ripped off the sleeves of his jersey during a nationally televised game against the New York Knicks in 2015.

In terms of footwear, players have used the NBA as a marketing platform for the various brands they endorse. The trend began in the 1980s when stars such as Julius Erving, Magic Johnson, Larry Bird, Michael Jordan, and Patrick Ewing endorsed their preferred shoe brands. Nike's Air Jordans were far and away the most popular basketball shoes (famously referred to as "kicks" by today's generation of players and fans) of that era.

Today's basketball shoe brands are diverse, to say the least. The most popular ones include the Nike Kobe 6 PROTRO, Nike PG 6, Nike Air Zoom GT Cut, Nike Kyrie 7, Nike KD 15, Nike Zoom Freak 4, Nike LeBron 20, Adidas Dame 8, Air Jordan 37, and New Balance TWO WXY V3. One thing's for sure: Nike is the dominant shoe brand in the National Basketball Association.

Despite the various accessories and shoes NBA players wear, NBA jersey rules, regulations and material remain constant variables they must follow. Prior to the 2017-18 NBA season, the home team wore lighter-colored uniforms while the visiting team wore dark-colored uniforms. However, the rule has changed: the home team can now wear any color it prefers as long as it's in contrast with the visiting team's jerseys.

The NBA also requires its players to wear their shorts one inch above their knees. The league also forbids them from wearing t-shirts underneath their jerseys. Several NBA teams currently allow their players to wear uniforms that show their sponsors' logos. In terms of composition, NBA jerseys are made of wicking material that absorbs sweat so the players compete at a high level without any inconvenience.

The NBA jersey has undergone a remarkable and colorful evolution since its inception in 1949. Players have sported many looks over the years that included skin-tight uniforms, short trousers, knee-high socks, headbands, mouth guards, arm bands, sleeved jerseys, and shoes. The league has kept up with the times and it will continue to do so in the next few years and beyond.

One of the trendsetters of the flappy shorts is arguably one of the greatest basketball players who ever laced up a pair of sneakers. We're talking about the legendary Michael Jordan, the so-called "GOAT" ("Greatest Of All Time"), who we will discuss in more detail in the next chapter.

Chapter 15:
THE GOAT: MICHAEL JORDAN

"Michael Jordan is one of those rare specimens that could have played any particular time and is a gifted athlete who's using those gifts in basketball, incredibly so. He has been the liaison between something that's not so good and making it great for all the rest. I think that almost every man in the NBA should give him 10% of their checks." – Wilt Chamberlain

Wilt Chamberlain, the only man to score 100 points in an NBA game, was one of the greatest basketball players of all time. However, he acknowledged that the Chicago Bulls' Michael Jordan was an exceptional player who could have given today's ballers serious competition. Whether it was Bill Russell's Boston Celtics or Tim Duncan's San Antonio Spurs, "MJ" could dominate the opposition like nobody else.

Basketball pundits have long debated who deserves the title of "GOAT" ("Greatest Of All Time") in the National Basketball Association: Michael Jordan, LeBron James, or Kobe Bryant. All three possess multiple MVP awards, multiple scoring titles, and multiple championship rings, in addition to having earned zealous acclaim from fans and commentators.

These guys also had similar playing styles, with uncanny abilities to score from anywhere on the court. Jordan, James, and Bryant also defied gravity, able to hang in the air and score against the toughest defenses imaginable. Plus, they were the media darlings of the NBA during their respective eras; MJ, "King James", and Kobe dominated headlines and secured endorsement deals galore.

Despite their similarities, Jordan has set himself apart from every NBA player past, present, and future. He won six NBA championships, five NBA MVP awards, and countless accolades. James, the league's all-time leading scorer, has four NBA titles and four NBA MVP awards, so is his closest pursuer. Unless James wins more MVP awards and NBA titles during the twilight of his NBA career, Jordan is still arguably the GOAT.

This brings me to ask: What made Michael Jordan an exceptional basketball player? Let's probe deeper into MJ's early life, career, and rise to superstardom so we can shed some light on that question.

Michael Jeffrey Jordan was born in Brooklyn, NY, on February 17, 1963. His father James was an equipment supervisor while his mother Deloris was a bank employee. He has two brothers, James and Larry, and two sisters, Deloris and Roslyn.

Although Jordan was born in New York because his father was on a work assignment, he spent his formative years in Wilmington, NC. Even at a young age, MJ had impressive athletic abilities. In fact, he was a three-sport star (basketball, baseball, and football) at Emsley A. Laney High School.

Michael was determined to make the Laney Buccaneers' basketball team. Unfortunately, his coaches thought he was too short (he stood 5'11" as a high school sophomore in 1979) so he didn't make the varsity squad. Instead, fellow sophomore Leroy Smith made the team.

It was one of the first major heartbreaks in Michael's life. But it was also motivation. He remained undaunted and vowed to become a better basketball player. He worked harder than ever before.

Jordan's hard work paid off. He didn't just make the varsity squad as a junior the following year, but he also became one of the best high school basketball players in the state of North Carolina. He averaged an impressive twenty-five points per game in his last two years of high school.

IN THE GAME

Michael's stock rose dramatically as his high school basketball career neared its conclusion. Many big-name college basketball programs including the North Carolina Tar Heels, Duke Blue Devils, South Carolina Gamecocks, Syracuse Orange, and Virginia Cavaliers sought to recruit him.

Jordan eventually accepted a basketball scholarship from Dean Smith's North Carolina Tar Heels prior to the 1982 NCAA season. Although Jordan was just a freshman, he gave basketball fans a glimpse of his otherworldly potential when he scored the game-winning shot against Patrick Ewing's Georgetown Hoyas in the 1982 NCAA title game. Jordan's Chicago Bulls and Ewing's New York Knicks eventually squared off in some memorable NBA playoff battles.

Jordan played three seasons for Smith, one of the greatest coaches in college basketball history. North Carolina had an impressive 83-20 (.805) win-loss record in Michael's three years with the team from 1982 to 1984. He averaged 17.7 points, 5.0 rebounds, and 1.8 assists in his college basketball career.

Jordan racked up a slew of accolades during his time with the Tar Heels, including:

- Two-time USA Basketball Male Athlete of the Year
- 1982 ACC Rookie of the Year
- Two-time Consensus First-Team All-American
- 1984 National College Player of the Year

Michael added another feather to his cap when he helped the United States men's basketball team win the gold medal in the 1984 Los Angeles Olympics. It was a fitting way to end his college basketball career and make the transition into the National Basketball Association.

The Chicago Bulls made Jordan the third overall selection of the 1984 NBA Draft. Michael was no ordinary rookie – he averaged 28.2 points, 6.5 rebounds, and 5.9 assists in his first year in the professional basketball ranks. He also earned the first of his eventual fourteen NBA All-Star Game appearances.

Jordan made an immediate impact on a Bulls team that missed the playoffs in five of the past six seasons prior to his arrival in the Windy City. Chicago evolved from playoff underdogs into perennial title contenders as Michael's NBA career soared to unprecedented heights.

Jordan ran into another stumbling block in his second year in the NBA. He broke his foot just three games into the 1985-86 NBA season and had to sit out the Bulls' next sixty-four games. Nevertheless, he returned in time for the playoffs where he torched Larry Bird's Boston Celtics for an unbelievable sixty-three points in the first round. The Celtics tried everything they possibly could to contain Jordan, to no avail.

Jordan became the Bulls' main man as he gained more experience in the NBA. He became their primary scoring option – he never averaged fewer than 26.9 points for the rest of his incredible NBA career with the Chicago Bulls.

Michael also had a killer instinct that few other players of his era possessed. One shining example was the decisive fifth game of the 1989 Eastern Conference first round playoff series against the Cleveland Cavaliers.

It was a seesaw affair for the most part. Jordan made a jumper to give the Bulls a precarious 99-98 lead with just six seconds left. The Cavaliers relinquished the lead on Craig Ehlo's layup three seconds later. That set the stage for Jordan's heroics.

Chicago's Brad Sellers inbounded the ball to Jordan. The latter made a move at the top of the key (a position on the court that has the free throw line and backboard parallel to one another) and made a buzzer-beating jump shot in Ehlo's face to give the Bulls a resounding 101-100 victory. NBA historians refer to it as "The Shot."

Jordan pumped his fist in jubilation as the horn sounded. It was an epic scene that sports documentaries have shown countless times over the years. The shocked Cavaliers fans were silent as Jordan and the Bulls moved to the second round of the playoffs.

Although the Bulls reached the Eastern Conference Finals in 1989 and 1990, they never got past their nemesis – Isiah Thomas' Detroit Pistons.

IN THE GAME

The Pistons, the so-called "Bad Boys" of the NBA, had a lineup that took no prisoners: they had Thomas, Joe Dumars, Vinnie "The Microwave" Johnson, Bill Laimbeer, Dennis Rodman, John Salley, and Rick Mahorn. They played a tenacious kind of defense that made Jordan bleed for his points (a term for working extremely hard to score in basketball) every time he got the ball. When MJ drove to the basket, the Pistons pummeled him and made sure he and the Bulls had no easy layups.

The Pistons stood in the way of the Bulls' championship aspirations as the NBA ushered in the 1990s. Detroit eventually won back-to-back NBA titles while MJ and the Bulls went home for the summer.

The 1990-91 edition of the Chicago Bulls ushered in a new era for the championship-hungry team. Jordan's supporting cast that season included Scottie Pippen, Horace Grant, B.J. Armstrong, Bill Cartwright, Craig Hodges, and John Paxson. Behind Jordan's 31.5-points-per-game average, Chicago won sixty-one games. Not only that, but they also swept the Pistons, their long-time adversaries, in the 1991 Eastern Conference Finals.

Jordan and Co. eventually beat Magic Johnson's Los Angeles Lakers 4-1 in the 1991 NBA Finals. MJ finally won his first title seven years after he entered the NBA. An emotional, beer-drenched Jordan sobbed while he hugged the Larry O'Brien trophy beside his father James in the Bulls' locker room.

MJ and the Bulls proved their championship was no fluke. Behind head coach Phil Jackson's exemplary leadership, they beat the Portland Trail Blazers and Phoenix Suns in consecutive years from 1992 to 1993 to secure their first 'three-peat' (winning three straight titles) during the Michael Jordan era.

Michael enjoyed the pinnacle of his professional basketball career in the early 1990s. Not only did he win several NBA titles, but he also helped his country continue its domination in international basketball.

After FIBA (the governing body of international basketball) allowed professional basketball players to represent their respective countries in 1992, USA Basketball formed one of the best teams in sports history – "The Dream Team." Jordan, Magic Johnson, Larry Bird, Scottie Pippen, Charles

Barkley, Karl Malone, Patrick Ewing, David Robinson, Clyde Drexler, Chris Mullin, John Stockton, and Christian Laettner easily won the gold medal in the 1992 Barcelona Olympics. It was MJ's second Olympic gold medal.

Just as Michael Jordan's pro basketball career reached incredible heights, he made a decision that shocked the world: he retired from the National Basketball Association on October 6, 1993. He had lost his passion for basketball. His father's death (two teenagers murdered James Jordan, Sr. at a North Carolina rest stop in the summer of 1993) played a major role in his decision.

Soon after MJ stepped down from the NBA, he pursued a minor-league baseball career. He played for the Birmingham Barons, the Double-A minor-league affiliate of the Chicago White Sox. Jordan struggled in his attempt at baseball, batting just .202 (.300 is the acceptable batting average) and led the Barons in strikeouts.

Major League Baseball's strike in the spring of 1995 discouraged Jordan from playing baseball – one of the sports he played as a youngster in North Carolina – again. He decided to return to the NBA in March 1995. It was a decision that made the Chicago Bulls the most dominant NBA team of the 1990s.

Behind the trio of Jordan, Scottie Pippen, and Dennis Rodman, Chicago won seventy-two games in the 1995-96 NBA season. At the time, that was a record, and it remained so until Stephen Curry's Golden State Warriors broke it with seventy-three wins twenty years later. Despite MJ's short hiatus from basketball, he still averaged 30.4 points per game that year. He showed no sign of rust whatsoever.

The Bulls beat the Seattle SuperSonics convincingly in the 1996 NBA Finals for their fourth NBA title. Chicago went up against the Utah Jazz in the NBA Finals in the next two years. Not even the legendary duo of John Stockton and Karl Malone (Jordan's teammates at the Barcelona Olympics several years earlier) could stop the Bulls juggernaut.

For his part, Jordan cemented his legacy as the GOAT in those two epic NBA Finals series against the Jazz. First, he carried the Bulls to an improbable

90-88 victory over the Jazz on the road in game five of the 1997 NBA Finals. Jordan scored thirty-eight points despite suffering from food poisoning. He felt so dehydrated it seemed he could not play on that day. According to Jordan's trainer Tim Grover, the Bulls star ate a pizza the night before the game, and he was in excruciating pain just several hours later.

Nonetheless, Jordan's incredible will to win prevailed. He scored fifteen points in the fourth quarter alone to lead the Bulls to a 3-2 series lead. A photo of Scottie Pippen assisting Jordan off the court late in the contest became one of the game's most iconic moments. Chicago went on to win the series and their fifth NBA title just two days later.

Jordan broke the Jazz's hearts again a year after his heroic effort. He made a clutch fifteen-foot jumper over Utah's Bryon Russell for an 87-86 triumph in game six of the 1998 NBA Finals. Jordan scored a game-high forty-five points (more than half of his team's production) to help clinch yet another three-peat and Chicago's sixth NBA championship. A jubilant MJ flashed six fingers to celebrate the historic moment on the Delta Center floor after the final buzzer went off.

Jordan announced his retirement from the NBA for a second time on January 13, 1999 while the league was in the midst of a player lockout. From Jordan's point of view, the imminent departures of Phil Jackson, Scottie Pippen, and Dennis Rodman, plus the Bulls' most recent three-peat, were clear indications it was time to step down from the NBA again. He left the game on a high note and on his own terms. At the time of MJ's second retirement, he was just one month short of his thirty-sixth birthday.

Jordan averaged 31.5 points, 6.3 rebounds, and 5.4 assists in a combined thirteen seasons with the Chicago Bulls from 1984 to 1998. His achievements with the Bulls include:

JORDAN'S ACHIEVEMENTS WITH CHICAGO BULLS

- 1985 NBA Rookie of the Year
- Two-time NBA Slam Dunk Contest champion

- Ten-time NBA scoring champion
- Six-time NBA champion
- Six-time NBA Finals Most Valuable Player
- Five-time NBA Most Valuable Player
- Twelve-time NBA All-Star
- Ten-time All-NBA First Team selection
- 1988 NBA Defensive Player of the Year
- Nine-time NBA All-Defensive First Team selection

Michael Jordan returned to the NBA just two weeks after the 9/11 attacks in New York City and Washington, D.C. He signed with the Washington Wizards prior to the 2001-02 NBA season and served as their director of basketball operations. MJ was thirty-eight years old when he came out of retirement for the second time in his iconic NBA career.

Even at a ripe old age by NBA standards, Jordan played better than many much younger than him. MJ averaged 21.2 points, 5.9 rebounds, and 4.4 assists in two seasons with Washington from 2001 to 2003. Better yet, Jordan made two more NBA All-Star Game appearances during his time in the nation's capital.

Despite Jordan's best efforts, the Wizards were a sub-par team that averaged just thirty-seven wins per season in his two years with the squad. Washington missed the playoffs for the fourteenth time in the past fifteen years prior to MJ's third and final retirement in the spring of 2003. Jordan was forty years old when he hung up his sneakers for good.

Michael Jordan is a member of the FIBA Hall of Fame, the North Carolina Sports Hall of Fame, the United States Olympic Hall of Fame, and the Naismith Memorial Basketball Hall of Fame. The Chicago Bulls retired his No. 23 jersey in 1994. He is also a member of the NBA 50th Anniversary Team and the NBA 75th Anniversary Team.

Jordan had numerous endorsements during his legendary basketball career. He endorsed brands such as Nike, McDonald's, Coca-Cola, Chevrolet, Gatorade, Ball Park Franks, Rayovac, Wheaties, Hanes, and MCI. His Nike Air Jordans are some of the best-selling sneakers in the world today. MJ credited his agent David Falk for his various endorsement deals.

Although it has been two decades since MJ retired from the NBA for a third and final time in 2003, he remains one of the most powerful business figures in the world. In fact, he earned a whopping $110 million from endorsement money alone in 2015. Forbes Magazine also pegged his net worth at an eye-popping $2 billion in 2023.

Jordan has remained involved in basketball during his retirement years. He became a minority owner of the Charlotte Bobcats on June 15, 2006 and became the team's majority owner four years later. The Bobcats became the Charlotte Hornets in Jordan's third year as their majority owner. Jordan eventually sold his majority stake with the team to Gabe Plotkin and Rick Schnall in 2023. He remains a minority owner of the Hornets.

Michael Jordan has also given back to the community throughout the years. He has raised money for charity via the Michael Jordan Celebrity Invitational golf tournament and Make-A-Wish-Foundation. When MJ turned sixty years old in 2023, he donated $10 million to the latter charity.

Let's take a look at twenty-three fun facts about the NBA's GOAT:

JORDAN FUN FACTS

- Had Jordan's basketball career not materialized, he would have become a weatherman. He has long been interested in geography and meteorology. In fact, he majored in cultural geography at the University of North Carolina.
- Jordan idolized Los Angeles Lakers point guard Earvin "Magic" Johnson during his high school and college days.
- One of MJ's best friends is a limousine driver named George Koehler, who picked him up at Chicago O'Hare International Airport prior to his rookie year in the NBA in 1984. It turned out the Chicago

Bulls forgot to send a driver to pick Jordan up at the airport. Koehler volunteered to give Jordan a ride. The two hit it off from the beginning. Michael eventually learned that Koehler went to the same school as his brother Larry. MJ and Koehler remain good friends to the present day.

- Jordan ate his pre-game meal approximately four hours before game time. His meal consisted of a 23-oz. New York steak, mashed or baked potatoes, salad, and ginger ale.
- Jordan's most famous nicknames were "MJ," "Air Jordan," and "His Airness."
- Jordan regularly stuck his tongue out whenever he drove to the basket. It was a tribute to his late father James who had a habit of sticking his tongue out during intense periods of work as an equipment supervisor.
- MJ had many memorable dunks in his NBA career. However, he considered his baseline tomahawk jam over the New York Knicks' Patrick Ewing at Madison Square Garden in 1991 his best of all time.
- Jordan never forgot his North Carolina roots. In fact, he always wore his North Carolina Tar Heels practice shorts underneath his regular NBA shorts when he played professional basketball from 1984 to 2003.
- Prior to Jordan's first retirement in 1993, a doctor (a staunch fanatic of MJ) named a type of salmonella virus *Salmonella mjordan* after him.
- Aside from MJ's famous No. 23, he also wore the numbers 12 and 45 during his iconic NBA career.
- Jordan and his first wife Juanita Vanoy had three children: Jeffrey, Marcus, and Jasmine.
- Both of Jordan's sons – Jeffrey and Marcus – played for the University of Central Florida Knights basketball team during their college days.

- Jordan and Vanoy divorced in December 2006.
- MJ is currently married to Cuban-American model Yvette Prieto. They exchanged vows in 2013. They have identical twin daughters named Victoria and Ysabel.
- Jordan has a four-year-old grandson Rakeem Michael courtesy of his daughter Jasmine.
- MJ's son-in-law is former Indiana Pacers forward Rakeem Christmas, the father of his grandson.
- Jordan became the first retired NBA player to become a majority team owner in 2010. He was also the first African-American majority owner of an NBA franchise.
- MJ was the lead actor in the 1996 Warner Bros. movie 'Space Jam.'
- Jordan began smoking cigars after he won his first NBA championship with the Chicago Bulls in 1991.
- One pair of MJ's Nike Air Jordan's sold for an insane $71,000 at an auction early in his NBA career.
- Jordan's Florida mansion has a basketball court, pool house, movie theater, and eleven bedrooms.

Michael Jordan is arguably the NBA's GOAT, not merely because of his numerous accomplishments and accolades. MJ was quite possibly the best player the NBA had ever seen because of his indomitable will to win – he never let any obstacle deter him from leading his Chicago Bulls to NBA championship glory.

In that regard, another NBA legend was made in the same mold: the Los Angeles Lakers' Kobe Bean Bryant. We will discuss Kobe's memorable NBA career in the next chapter.

Chapter 16:
REMEMBERING KOBE

"Many professional athletes are admired, praised, and cheered by the public for their inspiring athletic prowess. Sadly, most of these famous athletes are as temporary as snowmen... But some athletes are so special that they represent more than their athletic achievements. Kobe Bryant was such an athlete." – Kareem Abdul-Jabbar

Many athletes make an impact during their careers but quickly fade into oblivion after they retire. Who remembers guys such as David Thompson and Shawn Kemp nowadays? Hardly anybody. They're mere afterthoughts.

Thompson was a high-flying shooting guard who came to prominence by leading North Carolina State to the NCAA championship in 1974, after which he played professionally for the Denver Nuggets and Seattle SuperSonics from the mid-1970s to the mid-1980s. He could have been enshrined in the Naismith Memorial Basketball Hall of Fame in Springfield, MA. Instead, he struggled with drug issues and never reached his full potential.

Kemp was one of the most dominant power forwards of the early 1990s. I feel he was the best dunkers of his era – nobody could throw it down like he did. Whenever he caught alley-oop (a play when a player tosses the ball toward the basket and another player catches it for a dunk) passes from

Gary Payton in the Sonics' fastbreak attack, it was an easy slam dunk. I felt sorry for the basketball backboard – Kemp could easily shatter it with his insane power.

Shawn Kemp could have been one of the all-time greats. Unfortunately, his off-court issues tarnished his legacy.

Unlike Thompson and Kemp, Kobe Bryant was a different breed of NBA player. Abdul-Jabbar, the second-leading scorer in NBA history behind LeBron James, was right: Kobe transcended his athletic achievements.

Kobe Bean Bryant was born to parents Joe and Pamela Bryant in Philadelphia, PA on August 23, 1978. They got the name "Kobe" from the famous Japanese beef they saw on a menu. They derived their son's second name "Bean" from Joe's nickname "Jellybean." Kobe has two older sisters: Sharia and Shaya.

Kobe inherited his athletic genes and love for basketball from his dad Joe, an eight-year NBA veteran who played for the Houston Rockets, San Diego Clippers (now known as the Los Angeles Clippers), and his hometown Philadelphia 76ers in the mid-1970s and early 1980s. Kobe learned to play hoops when he was just three years old and he never looked back. Although he spent his formative years in Philadelphia, his favorite NBA team was the Los Angeles Lakers.

Joe retired from the NBA when Kobe was six years old. The older Bryant continued playing professional basketball in Europe after he left the NBA. He played in Italy for the next seven years. Consequently, Kobe, his only son, would learn to embrace the Italian way of life.

Kobe honed his basketball skills when the Bryant family moved to Reggio Emilia, a city in Northern Italy. He studied films of NBA games his grandfather mailed from the United States – a skill he would put to good use when he played in the National Basketball Association for twenty years. Kobe also watched European sports cartoons to expand his knowledge of basketball during his youth.

Joe Bryant played for the Italian professional basketball team Olimpia Basket Pistola as the 1980s wound down. Kobe, who was in grade school, worked as a ball boy for the team. Joe Bryant's teammate, Leon Douglas, marveled at Kobe's insane work ethic – the kid practiced his shots relentlessly at halftime. The players had to shoo him away so he would stop. It was a sign of things to come for Kobe: nobody matched his legendary work ethic in the National Basketball Association several years later.

Kobe also developed a passion for soccer during his time in Europe. In fact, he became a fan of the Italian Serie A club A.C. Milan when he was in grade school. Not only that, but Kobe also became fluent in the Italian language, a trait that set him apart from his NBA contemporaries.

The Bryant family returned to Philadelphia when Kobe was thirteen years old in 1991. After Kobe graduated from Bala Cynwyd Middle School, he enrolled at Lower Merion High School. Kobe made the Lower Merion Aces varsity squad as a freshman in 1992. He made an instant impact and became one of the best high school basketball players in the country.

The Aces got off to a rough start with Kobe on their roster. They won just four of twenty-four games during his freshman season. Undaunted, Kobe took his game to new heights and turned the Aces into perennial contenders in the next three years. With Kobe leading the charge, Lower Merion High became a juggernaut that won seventy-seven of ninety games from 1993 to 1995.

Kobe became a thirty-point scorer who could also excel on the defensive end. He wasn't just a two-way player (a baller who excels in both offense and defense); he also became a man among boys. He was so good, some basketball experts thought he could play in the National Basketball Association straight out of high school.

Kobe made a strong case for himself as an NBA prospect. He finished his outstanding high school basketball career with 2,883 career points. His point total surpassed those of NBA stars Wilt Chamberlain (who once scored 100 points in an NBA game) and Lionel "L-Train" Simmons.

Bryant earned several accolades as a member of the Lower Merion Aces, including:

- Naismith High School Player of the Year.

IN THE GAME

- Gatorade Men's National Basketball Player of the Year.
- McDonald's All-American.
- First-Team Parade All-American.
- *USA TODAY* All-USA First team selection.

It was a mere taste of things to come for the seventeen-year-old teen basketball sensation. Although many big-name college basketball programs such as the Duke Blue Devils, North Carolina Tar Heels, Michigan Wolverines, and Villanova Wildcats recruited him hard, he eventually turned them down and declared for the 1996 NBA Draft. Kobe entertained thoughts of turning pro when another high school basketball standout, Kevin Garnett, entered the NBA ranks one year earlier.

Kobe worked with the team he grew up following, the Los Angeles Lakers, in the weeks prior to the 1996 NBA Draft. Lakers' general manager, Jerry West, knew Bryant was their guy the moment he scrimmaged with them.

West and Co. orchestrated a trade with the Charlotte Hornets, who took Bryant with the thirteenth overall selection. Charlotte traded Kobe to Los Angeles in exchange for veteran center Vlade Divac on July 9, 1996. It was surreal but true – Kobe Bryant was officially a Los Angeles Laker. Better yet, Kobe joined forces with former Orlando Magic center Shaquille O'Neal, who the Lakers acquired in the off-season. The duo would eventually help the Purple and Gold win three NBA titles in the early 2000s.

Although Bryant was just eighteen years old when he joined the Lakers, he had the full basketball arsenal. He patterned his game after those of several NBA greats.

"Michael Jordan's post-up, Reggie Miller's step-back," he once said (via *The Athletic's* Rhiannon Walker), "Little pieces and bits of every player; I'll take it and add to my game."

It didn't take long for Kobe to make NBA history. At eighteen years, five months, and five days old, he became the league's youngest starter on January 28, 1997. He got the opportunity after starting small forward Robert Horry sprained his left ankle. Bryant wasn't nervous at all. In fact, he took a nap in the locker room prior to tip-off against the Dallas Mavericks.

Kobe's performance in that game was astounding, netting him twelve points, three rebounds, two assists, and two steals in a 102-83 trouncing of Dallas. He averaged 7.6 points per game as a rookie, and helped the Lakers win fifty-six games in the first year of the Kobe-Shaq era in Los Angeles. The Lakers eventually made the playoffs sixteen times in Kobe's twenty seasons in Southern California.

Like many in his generation, Kobe idolized Michael Jordan. Over the years, Jordan's influence on Bryant's playing style became increasingly apparent. He modeled his game, approach, and attitude after MJ's. The 1998 All-Star Game at Madison Square Garden in New York gave us an indication of Kobe's desire to follow in Jordan's sneaker-prints.

The 19-year-old Kobe, a first-time All-Star, and the 34-year-old Jordan, in his last All-Star appearance as a Chicago Bull, went one-on-one several times. Bryant showboated a bit, unleashing moves like 360 dunks, to which Jordan was no stranger. MJ was fully cognizant of the fact that Kobe sought to exploit Jordan's likely weakness from a recent illness. Consequently, Jordan compensated with an incredible outpouring of energy, and the contest became one between the man who originated a set of tactics, and the man advancing them into the future.

The Eastern Conference won, and Jordan's 23 points made him the game's MVP. Kobe was the second-highest scorer, with 18. The torch wasn't passed just yet, but it was about to be.

Kobe steadily increased his scoring average to 19.9 points in his fourth year in the NBA in the 1999-2000 season. With Kobe firing on all cylinders, the Lakers were a juggernaut that won sixty-seven games that year. Bryant also reached the NBA Finals for the first time in his legendary professional basketball career. The Lakers squared off against an upstart Indiana Pacers team led by a player Kobe patterned his step-back jumper after – Reggie Miller.

The Lakers hadn't won an NBA title since 1988, so they wanted to end their twelve-year title drought. It didn't come easy, because the Pacers were seeking their first NBA title since they joined the NBA in 1976. Kobe wasn't going to be denied, though.

Although Bryant sprained his ankle in game two and sat out game three, he single-handedly carried the Lakers to victory in game four. He scored twenty-two points in the second half to lead Los Angeles to an exciting 120-118 overtime victory over Indiana. The Lakers eventually beat the Pacers in six games to clinch their twelfth NBA championship. For his part, Kobe Bryant earned the first of his eventual five NBA championship rings.

The Lakers became a dynasty over the next five seasons. They averaged fifty-five wins and won two more NBA titles from 2001 to 2004. At this point in Kobe's career, he was a legitimate scoring threat who averaged more than twenty-five points per game. Bryant, Shaq, and head coach Phil Jackson were instrumental in leading the Lakers to a three-peat from 2000 to 2002.

Kobe's career was not without controversy. At its most serious, there were the sexual assault allegations which surfaced in the summer of 2003, around an incident in Colorado. The trial occurred during the following season. Bryant had to make regular trips away from the team and then back, in order to be ready by game time. The case was dropped after Bryant's accuser refused to testify in the case.

A long-simmering rift between Kobe and Shaq grew larger in that 2003-04 season, coming to a head in the wake of L.A.'s disappointing loss to the Pistons in the Finals. Bryant was set to be a free agent, and there were rumors he was planning to jump to the Los Angeles Clippers. The contract for head coach Phil Jackson, a favorite of O'Neal's, was not renewed. Shaq soon demanded a trade, and got his wish. He was sent to the Miami Heat, and Kobe was now a lone superstar in the Lakers.

Naturally, the Lakers took a huge step backward when O'Neal departed. Consequently, Kobe bore the brunt of the offense. Although he averaged 24.0 points per game that year, the Lakers won just thirty-four games – it was their worst showing since the 1993-94 season when they won just thirty-three games.

Although the Lakers won an average of forty-three games from 2005 to 2006, they lost in the first round of the playoffs each time. Kobe continued playing the best basketball of his NBA career–he averaged a lofty 33.0 points per game during that two-year stretch. The highlight was Bryant's eighty-one-point outburst against the Toronto Raptors on January 22, 2006. It was the second-highest individual scoring output in NBA history behind Wilt Chamberlain's 100-point game on March 2, 1962.

Bryant was the undisputed leader of the Lakers since O'Neal left for South Florida. The former wasn't content with the Lakers being mere first-round exits. As the 2000s wound down, Los Angeles had a formidable core that included Bryant, Lamar Odom, Pau Gasol, Derek Fisher, and Metta World Peace (formerly Ron Artest).

Bryant and Co. won fifty-seven games in the 2007-08 NBA season. Unfortunately, they lost to the Boston Celtics, their long-time nemesis, in six games in the 2008 NBA Finals. The Celtics' vaunted trio of Paul Pierce, Kevin Garnett, and Ray Allen were too much for the Lakers to handle.

The Lakers won an average of sixty-two games in the next two seasons. With Kobe (who was now in his early thirties) averaging thirty points per game in the post-season, Los Angeles did something it had never done since the 2001-02 NBA season – win consecutive NBA titles. The Lakers beat the Orlando Magic in five games in 2009.

On the other hand, they beat the Celtics in an NBA Finals rematch in seven games one year later. After Boston's defense converged on Bryant, Kobe found a wide-open Metta World Peace for the series-clinching three-pointer with just one minute remaining in game seven. Although Kobe didn't shoot well (he made just six of twenty-four field-goal attempts in game seven), he scored twenty-three points and earned NBA Finals MVP honors for the second straight year. Kobe also earned his fifth NBA championship ring.

When Bryant turned thirty years old, he enjoyed the pinnacle of his basketball career. Not only did he help the Lakers win back-to-back NBA titles, but he also helped Team USA win the gold medal in men's basketball in the

IN THE GAME

2008 Beijing Olympics. Kobe won another gold medal four years later at the 2012 London Olympics.

Regrettably, Kobe's NBA career began its downward trajectory after he earned his last NBA championship. The Lakers won fifty-seven games in Phil Jackson's final season as their head coach in the 2010-11 NBA season. Despite this impressive win total, Los Angeles never made it past the second round of the playoffs.

The Lakers gradually felt the effects of Jackson's departure in subsequent seasons. They won an average of forty-three games under new head coach Mike Brown in the next two seasons. However, they never made it past the second round of the post-season. Los Angeles didn't fare better with head coaches Mike D'Antoni and Byron Scott in the next three seasons: the Lakers' win total dipped from twenty-seven in 2014 to an abysmal seventeen games in 2016. Their 17-65 win-loss record in the 2015-16 season was their worst since they moved to Los Angeles, CA, from Minneapolis, MN, in 1960.

For his part, Kobe, the man known as "The Black Mamba," signed a two-year contract extension worth approximately $48.5 million on November 25, 2013. That contract made him the highest-paid player in the National Basketball Association. Although Kobe enjoyed his hefty paycheck, a knee injury limited him to just six games in the 2013-14 NBA season.

Bryant re-wrote the NBA record books in his nineteenth NBA season several months later. He had thirty-one points, twelve rebounds, and eleven assists in a 129-122 win over the Toronto Raptors (the team he had scorched for eighty-one points more than eight years earlier) on November 30, 2014. The thirty-six-year-old Lakers guard became the oldest player to score at least thirty points and record ten rebounds and ten assists in a game.

Kobe set another NBA record when he became the league's leading scorer in a 100-94 triumph over the Minnesota Timberwolves just twenty-four days later. Bryant surpassed the great Michael Jordan (32,292 career points) on December 14, 2014. Kobe is currently fourth on the NBA's all-time scoring list with 33,643 career points.

Bryant's good fortune did not last long. He tore his rotator cuff while attempting a two-handed slam dunk against the New Orleans Pelicans on January 21, 2015. Kobe underwent season-ending shoulder surgery several days later. With Bryant out for the rest of the season, the Lakers stumbled to a 21-61 win-loss record under first-year head coach Byron Scott, one of the mainstays of the legendary "Lake Show" era of the 1980s.

Bryant eventually recovered from his rotator cuff tear and played sixty-six games for the Lakers in his twentieth and final NBA season. The thirty-seven-year-old legend averaged 17.6 points, 3.7 rebounds, and 2.8 assists in the 2015-16 NBA campaign. Although they were modest numbers, he ended his professional basketball career on a strong note. He scored sixty points in a 101-96 win over the Utah Jazz in his final NBA game on April 13, 2016. The Black Mamba officially signed off.

Kobe Bryant averaged 25.0 points, 5.2 rebounds, and 4.7 assists in his NBA career from 1996 to 2015. His many basketball-related achievements include:

- 1997 NBA Slam Dunk Contest Champion.
- Five-time NBA champion.
- Two-time NBA Finals MVP.
- 2009 NBA MVP.
- Two-time NBA scoring champion.
- Eighteen-time NBA All-Star.
- Eleven-time All-NBA First Team selection.
- Two-time All-NBA Second Team selection.
- Two-time All-NBA Third Team selection.
- Nine-time NBA All-Defensive First Team selection.
- Three-time NBA All-Defensive Second Team selection.

The Los Angeles Lakers also retired his No. 8 and No. 24 jerseys on December 19, 2017.

IN THE GAME

Let's check out the ten most memorable moments of Kobe Bryant's legendary basketball career:

KOBE'S CAREER

- **Posterizing Ben Wallace, 1996**: 'Posterizing' is a basketball term which means another player dunks on you in a vicious manner – photographers snap their cameras simultaneously at that moment. Magazines and publications show that dunk on their posters (hence the term 'posterizing') shortly afterward. That's exactly what Kobe Bryant did to his fellow rookie Ben Wallace of the then-Washington Bullets in NBA Summer League play in 1996. It was a mere glimpse of what became an outstanding twenty-year NBA career.

- **Youngest player to start an NBA game, 1997**: Although young eighteen-year-old Kobe Bryant started off slowly in his professional basketball career (he averaged just 7.6 points as a rookie in 1996), he re-wrote the NBA record books just five months after entering the league. At just eighteen years, five months, and five days old, Kobe made his first NBA start against the Dallas Mavericks in January 1997. He became the youngest baller in league history to do that.

- **First fifty-point game, 2000**: Bryant became the Los Angeles Lakers' main weapon on offense as his NBA career progressed. Although Kobe was still playing in Shaquille O'Neal's shadow in the 2000 NBA season, he proved he was a big-time scorer when he recorded his first career fifty-point game against the Golden State Warriors that year. It certainly wasn't his last.

- **Alley-oop pass[3] to Shaq, 2000**: Kobe Bryant was known more for his scoring prowess and high-wire acts than his passing abilities during his NBA career. Nevertheless, his perfectly timed pass to Shaquille O'Neal for the series-clinching dunk against the Portland Trail Blazers in game seven of the 2000 Western Conference Finals

---

3   An 'alley-oop' is a scoring opportunity where a player tosses the ball into the air. One of his teammates jumps high to catch and dunk the ball in one swift motion

showed another dimension of his deadly arsenal.

- **Stepping up in game four of the 2000 NBA Finals**: Bryant had to pick up the slack for Shaquille O'Neal in game four of the 2000 NBA Finals against the Indiana Pacers. O'Neal fouled out in overtime, so Bryant carried the Lakers on his back. Shaking off the effects of an injured ankle that forced him to sit out game three, twenty-one-year-old Kobe proved he was mature for his age – he scored six of his twenty-eight points in overtime to propel the Lakers to a 120-118 victory and a 3-1 series lead.

- **Eighty-one-point game against the Raptors, 2006**: Many NBA historians believe nobody will ever surpass Wilt Chamberlain's historic 100-point game on March 2, 1962. Although nobody has broken that record, Kobe Bryant came closest to displacing "The Big Dipper" in the NBA record books.

- **Clinching his first NBA title without Shaq**: When the Lakers reached the 2009 NBA Finals against the Orlando Magic in 2009, it had been four years since Shaquille O'Neal left for the Miami Heat. Some NBA experts questioned Bryant's ability to lead the Lakers to an NBA championship without Shaq. Kobe put those speculations to rest when he scored 30 points in the decisive game five of the 2009 NBA Finals and lifted the Purple and Gold to their fifteenth NBA title in franchise history.

- **Winning his second Olympic gold medal, 2012**: Only a select few NBA players get to represent the United States in Olympic competition. Bryant won Olympic gold for his country in the 2008 Beijing Olympics and 2012 London Olympics. With Kobe firing on all cylinders for Team USA, the Americans proved they are truly the gold standard of men's basketball.

- **Becoming the NBA's all-time leading scorer, 2014**: Thirty-six-year-old Kobe Bryant scored his 32,292nd NBA point (the most in league history at the time) in a game against the Minnesota Timberwolves on December 14, 2014. Bryant's 33,643 career points currently ranks him fourth in league history behind LeBron James, Kareem Abdul-Jabbar, and Karl Malone.

- **Sixty-point finale, 2016**: Although Kobe was hampered by various injuries during the latter part of his twenty-year NBA career, the thirty-seven-year-old legend showed everyone he was far from washed up when he scored an incredible sixty points in his final NBA game against the Utah Jazz in April 2016. If anybody knew how to end his pro basketball career on a high note, it was Kobe Bean Bryant.

Kobe Bryant was one of the most popular NBA players of his era. He had endorsements with Adidas, Coca-Cola, McDonald's, Spalding, Upper Deck, Nutella, Turkish Airlines, and Nike.

After he retired from the National Basketball Association in 2016, Kobe dabbled in filmmaking and television. He created and wrote the television series *Musecage* and *Detail* for ESPN and ESPN+ in 2017 and 2018, respectively. Bryant won the Academy Award for Best Animated Short Film as the writer and executive producer of the full-length animated feature film *Dear Basketball* in 2018. He became the first African American to accomplish the feat.

Kobe and his wife Vanessa have four daughters: Natalia, Gianna, Bianka, and Capri. Kobe was a staunch fanatic of the NFL's Philadelphia Eagles, his hometown team. Bryant's video that showed him celebrating the Eagles' historic win in Super Bowl LII in February 2018 went viral on social media. Kobe pumped his fist and screamed with delight while carrying his third daughter Bianka in his Southern California home.

Sadly, Kobe Bryant, one of the greatest NBA players of his generation, was killed in a tragic helicopter crash on January 26, 2020. The accident also claimed the lives of his thirteen-year-old daughter Gianna and seven other people on board the chopper. Kobe Bryant was forty-one years old at the time of his death.

"When Kobe Bryant died, a piece of me died," Michael Jordan said in a tribute to the fallen Black Mamba at the Staples Center in Los Angeles, CA on February 25, 2020.

It bears repeating: Kobe Bean Bryant transcended his NBA achievements. Even Michael Jordan acknowledged that Bryant's death affected him deeply. Although Kobe is no longer with us, we will always remember the tremendous impact he made on basketball fans all over the world.

"Around the world" isn't hyperbole, either. We've already discussed the international impact of Olympic basketball, but there's also a global aspect which is increasingly reflected in the NBA, itself. Nobody has better represented that aspect than Yao Ming, who we'll discuss in the next chapter.

Chapter 17
THE RISE OF YAO MING AND THE ASIAN INFLUENCE

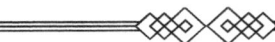

The boom of the NBA's popularity during the 1980s and beyond had many aftereffects. One is the globalization of the sport.

Basketball now has a significant presence and following in China, making it one of the league's most important international markets. The popularity soared in the 1990s and 2000s, largely due to the success of players like Yao Ming in the NBA, and the accomplishments of the national team in international competitions, including the Olympic Games.

But the origins of basketball in China go even further back. The Young Men's Christian Association (YMCA) brought basketball to China in 1895. It spread quickly enough that it was an event in the country's National Games only fifteen years later. By 1935, basketball was voted by the citizens to be one of the two national sports, alongside ping pong.

After the formation of the People's Republic of China in the late 1940s, sports such as basketball were a way to foster diplomatic relations. When the PRC captured its first Olympic medal in the 1984 games in Los Angeles, after the women's team took the bronze medal by defeating Canada, it was a moment of legitimization for the nation.

The cliche goes that Yao Ming was, and is, larger than life. In exact terms, he is 7'6". But after successful professional careers in his home nation and in the NBA, his influence and reach stretch worldwide.

He joined the Shanghai Sharks of the Chinese Basketball Association (CBA) as a teenager – first on the junior team and eventually (after four seasons) on the senior team. In his rookie year on the senior club, he averaged 10 points and 8 rebounds a game. A broken foot the next year limited his jumping ability, and was a precursor of injuries to come.

But the ensuing seasons were where Yao really broke out into a full-fledged superstar. He helped Shanghai reach the CBA Finals in 2001. After Wang Zhizhi of the rival Bayi Rockets left to become the first Chinese player to enter the NBA, the Sharks won their first title. During the playoffs, he averaged 38.9 points and 20.2 rebounds a game, while shooting 76.6% from the field.

Soon, the NBA would come calling for Yao. His entrance into the league was highly anticipated due to his size, skill, and far-reaching impact. He possessed a rare combination of height, agility, and all-around talent.

The Houston Rockets had the top pick in the 2002 NBA Draft and made Yao the first international player without prior American college experience to be selected first overall. It was a monumental step in increasing the popularity of the sport as a whole, but also specifically of the NBA in China. And it made the Rockets an instant favorite with the citizens.

Yao played nine seasons in the NBA – each of them with Houston. He was named an All-Star eight times, twice was named to the All-NBA Second Team, and three times chosen for the All-NBA Third Team. He averaged 19 points, 9.2 rebounds, and nearly two blocks per game. Yao's Rockets never got very far in the playoffs, and Yao himself struggled to make it through each season due to injuries.

Still, he was one of the most dominant centers during his time. During his NBA career, he found time to represent his country in international competitions, and was even a three-time gold medalist and three-time MVP at the FIBA Asia Championships.

IN THE GAME

As much as his on-court impact was significant, his off-court impact – bridging the gap between the NBA and Chinese basketball – has been invaluable. He was a cultural and physical phenomenon, with the personality required to balance the demands of playing in a foreign land, on the biggest stage, while bridging the social, economic, and political landscapes of two very different worlds.

For all those reasons, Yao entered the Basketball Hall of Fame in 2016, and his number 11 was retired by the Rockets. He is currently the proprietor of a well-regarded winery in Napa Valley, California.

The effects of Yao's presence are still felt. The NBA has secured lucrative broadcasting deals in China, allowing millions of fans to watch games on television and streaming platforms. The league also has a strong presence on Chinese social media, engaging fans with content in Mandarin.

The league has partnered with Chinese companies and brands to promote basketball and its stars in China. This includes endorsements, merchandise sales, and sponsorships, which have helped raise the league's profile and drive revenue.

The NBA regularly hosts preseason games and events in China, including the NBA China Games and NBA Global Games, bringing top teams and players to local cities and further connecting with local fans.

The NBA has invested in basketball development programs there, supporting youth leagues, training camps, and coaching clinics to nurture talent and grow the sport at the grassroots level.

But in spite of this popularity boom, the NBA's relationship with China has not always been smooth.

In 2019, a tweet by Rockets General Manager Daryl Morey in support of pro-democracy protesters in Hong Kong sparked a backlash from Chinese authorities, and led to strained relations between the NBA and China. However, the league continues to prioritize its presence in the Chinese market, recognizing its importance both commercially and culturally.

Nevertheless, Yao – who has since become the president of the Chinese

Basketball Association – asserts that the alliance is not broken.

"The NBA is in the first class," Yao said. "The players, the teams are all still very well welcome in China."

Recent examples include Minnesota Timberwolves forward Kyle Anderson competing with China at the FIBA World Cup, while Miami Heat All-Star Jimmy Butler embarked on a tour of the country one summer.

"The game has inspired billions of people around the world," Yao said in his Hall of Fame induction speech. "As one of them I will do my part to continue to grow the great game of basketball. We are all looking forward to see the stars of tomorrow emerge and shine."

Despite a shortened NBA career, Yao Ming is one of the greatest and most impactful success stories in the history of basketball. Conversely, there have also been a share of tragedies on the court, which we will discuss in the next chapter.

Chapter 18:
WHEN THE GAME GETS REAL: MEDICAL EMERGENCIES AND TRAGEDIES ON THE COURT

The basketball court can be a place of great triumph, but it can also turn quickly into a scene of tragedy and terror. It's hard to fathom that a place where many lifelong dreams are born is also the same place where some dreams quickly fade away. I know it's ironic, but that is the harsh reality of basketball and sports.

Hey, ballers are human, too. Despite their superstar status, they can sustain injuries while playing. Let's break down some of the most common basketball-related injuries:

- **Ankle sprains**: Ankle sprains are among the most frequent injuries players deal with. Whenever a baller takes a shot or grabs a rebound, he may turn his ankle sideways and consequently suffer a sprained ankle.

    NBA or NCAA television broadcasts usually show ankle injuries in slow motion. Take a closer look when that happens – you will have an idea of how painful it is just by looking at how the player sprained his ankle. One of the best ways to treat ankle sprains is by immersing the player's foot in a bucket of ice to help decrease swelling in the affected area.

- **Jammed fingers**: Another common basketball injury is jammed fingers. As the term implies, it happens when the ball makes direct contact with the tip of a player's finger. This makes the finger's joint swell considerably. In extreme cases, the ball makes a player's finger bend backwards or sideways. Notice many players wear finger bands to prevent jammed fingers. Ice treatment and finger splints help heal this basketball injury.

- **Knee injuries**: Playing basketball requires abrupt and explosive movements that take a toll on players' knees. An anterior cruciate ligament (ACL) tear is one of the most serious injuries in basketball. The ACL is the tissue that connects the thigh bone to the shinbone. When a player hears a popping sound from his knee after he makes an explosive movement on the court, that is an ominous warning sign.

  Players who sustain serious ACL tears typically undergo surgery and intense rehabilitation. It will take them several months before they can play again. Some ACL tears are so severe that players miss one full season.

- **Deep thigh bruising**: Basketball is a physical sport. It entails contact, especially if you attempt a lay-up against a physical team or you try posting up (trying to score against an opponent with your back to the basket within a ten-foot radius of the hoop). Although basketball isn't as physical as boxing, mixed martial arts, rugby, or American football, it's inevitable other players will clobber you, especially when the game is on the line.

  When a player bruises his thigh, doctors typically recommend ice to help relieve the discomfort. They're not as serious as ACL tears – many players usually play again after missing only a few minutes of action. Some players wear girdles with thigh pads to prevent deep thigh bruising.

- **Facial cuts**:

  Facial cuts are another common basketball injury. Power forwards or centers who grab rebounds flail their elbows, so if an opponent gets in the way, they may get hit and suffer a facial cut. Players can also get facial cuts when an opponent tries to foul them by making contact with their body. An arm makes inadvertent contact with a face, and before you know it, blood begins to ooze from a facial cut.

  Trainers and team physicians typically dab the affected area with a towel to stop the bleeding. In extreme cases, they stitch a player up so he can continue playing. Facial cuts rarely keep players out for prolonged periods of time.

- **Stress fractures**: These are small cracks in bones that typically stem from overuse or repetitive movements. Basketball players usually develop stress fractures in their lower legs or feet. Doctors immobilize the affected area and recommend players to avoid placing excess weight on it. Physicians give players the signal to return to action once the stress fracture heals completely.

  In some cases, players suffer more than just a mere stress fracture. Indiana Pacers forward Paul George sustained one of the most serious and gruesome injuries in basketball history in the summer of 2014.

  George was part of a Team USA basketball scrimmage in Las Vegas, NV for the upcoming 2014 FIBA Basketball World Cup. The White Team's James Harden was about to score on a fastbreak play when George tried to challenge his lay-up attempt. Unfortunately, George jammed his right foot on the basketball stanchion (the padded base of the basketball hoop). Consequently, Paul's lower leg bent at a 90-degree angle and he broke his lower leg bone instantly.

  Although George missed most of the 2014-15 NBA campaign, he made a full recovery after undergoing surgery and rehabilitation during the off-season. George is currently part of a Los Angeles Clippers core that includes Kawhi Leonard and Russell Westbrook.

Basketball-related issues aren't limited to the above-mentioned injuries. In fact, college basketball players have a higher incidence of sudden cardiac death than previously thought. According to a study published by the *American Heart Association Journal Circulation* on May 14, 2023, male African-American college basketball players are especially at risk.

On an even more alarming note, basketball players in general are highly susceptible to sudden cardiac death (also known as SCD, it's the sudden breakdown of cardiac activity that stems from an irregular heart rhythm), according to UAB Medicine's official website.

Dr. Sara Gould, who previously served as a team physician for the UAB Blazers women's basketball team and at several NBA events, told UAB-Medicine.org the sudden and explosive movements basketball players make may actually compromise their cardiovascular systems:

"Male basketball players are the most likely athletes to suffer sudden cardiac death. First of all, basketball requires sudden bursts of cardiovascular effort that may expose heart disorders. Also, the body type of athletes selected for basketball – tall with long limbs – seems to increase the likelihood for connective tissue disorders that can affect the heart."

To demonstrate Gould's point, 132 young basketball players from the middle school, high school, and college ranks in the United States had cardiac arrests during a two-year span from 2014 to 2016. If you thought only older people who smoke, eat processed food, and don't exercise are susceptible to cardiac arrest, think again – young ballers are also at risk.

As I write this chapter, memories of Hank Gathers and Reggie Lewis – two of the most tragic cardiac-related deaths in basketball history – come to mind.

Gathers was the best player of a Loyola Marymount Lions team of the late 1980s and early 1990s. He was a 6'7" left-handed power forward who averaged 23.3 points and 9.6 rebounds in his four-year NCAA basketball career. His 32.7 points and 13.7 rebounds per game led all college basketball players in 1989.

Tragedy struck in Gathers' senior season. He collapsed near mid-court within the vicinity of teammate Erik Spoelstra (the current head coach of the NBA's Miami Heat) during a WCC semifinal game against the Portland Pilots on March 4, 1990. Gathers had scored on an alley-oop dunk to give Loyola Marymount a twelve-point lead just thirteen seconds earlier.

"The absolute silence in the gym after he fell..." Spoelstra told ESPN Insider Nick Gasaway thirty-one years later. "It's something I'll never forget."

Gathers shortly stopped breathing and died at Marina Del Ray Hospital later that evening. He was just twenty-three years old at the time of his death. An autopsy revealed Gathers had hypertrophic cardiomyopathy (a thickened heart).

Gasaway cited a cardiologist who was featured in a *Los Angeles Times* article in the wake of Gathers' death. The doctor told the newspaper he warned Gathers to stop playing basketball and exercising after he had a fainting spell just three months earlier. Gathers refused to listen.

Reggie Lewis, a rising star of the NBA's Boston Celtics, also succumbed to heart issues just three-and-a-half years after Gathers' death. Lewis was part of an aging Celtics core in the early 1990s that included Robert Parish, Kevin McHale, Larry Bird, Kevin Gamble, and Dee Brown.

Just how good was Reggie? According to ESPN Senior Writer Jackie MacMullan, Lewis was one of just six players who had 7,500 points, 1,500 rebounds, 1,000 assists, and 500 steals from 1989 to 1993. The other five ballers were Charles Barkley, Clyde Drexler, Michael Jordan, Karl Malone, and Chris Mullin – members of the "Dream Team" that won the gold medal in the 1992 Barcelona Olympics. All five men are enshrined in the Naismith Memorial Basketball Hall of Fame in Springfield, MA.

Lewis could also play tough, in-your-face defense – he blocked the great Michael Jordan four times and made the latter miss twenty-four of his thirty-six shot attempts on March 31, 1991.

"He was on his way to being one of the best two-guards (shooting guards) in the league," Lewis' teammate Brian Shaw told ESPN.

Sadly, Lewis could have been part of that elite group. Regrettably, his promising NBA career was tragically cut short.

One of the first warning signs manifested during a playoff game against the Charlotte Hornets in the spring of 1993. Lewis inexplicably fell while he was running down the court. No other players were within his immediate vicinity.

Lewis couldn't explain what had just happened. Twenty years later, MacMullan still remembered the dazed look on Reggie's face when he walked to the Celtics' bench.

Lewis was shooting baskets with a friend at Brandeis University in the summer of 1993. Just like Gathers, Lewis also received advice from his doctors warning him not to push himself too hard on the basketball court.

After shooting for one hour, Lewis, collapsed and was short of breath. Doctors declared Reggie dead just two hours later. He was just twenty-eight years old.

Lewis' untimely death was eerily similar to that of "Pistol" Pete Maravich, a showman (a flamboyant player) of the 1970s NBA who mesmerized fans with his fancy passes and trick shots. Maravich died due to a heart attack while he was playing a basketball scrimmage game at the Pasadena First Church in California in January 1988. "The Pistol" passed away at just forty years of age.

Although the basketball court has had its share of horrific health tragedies and injuries over the years, the good has outweighed the bad. Basketball remains one of the most popular and exciting team sports in the world. In my humble opinion, no shot makes it more exciting than the slam dunk. We will discuss the art of this gravity-defying shot in more detail in the next chapter.

Chapter 19:
THE ART OF SLAM DUNKS

Sure, a three-pointer or an acrobatic shot can make the crowd get up on its feet. However, the slam dunk does more than just excite the crowd. Think of how an exclamation mark makes a sentence more emphatic. That's what the slam dunk does: it sends a strong message to the other team and the people watching on television or live at the stadium. It's the dunker's way of telling the guy guarding him, "You can't keep me in check." It's also the dunker's way of pumping up the crowd, especially at the end of his team's scintillating scoring binge.

What exactly is a slam dunk? It's a shot where a player jumps up and forces the ball into the basket either with one or two hands. It's a shot that defies the laws of gravity.

I remember watching Vince Carter dunk over the 7'2" Frenchman Frederic Weis in the 2000 Sydney Olympics. Although I am not a Toronto Raptors fan, I yelled in excitement after seeing Vince posterize Weis – I had not seen anything like it before. If you haven't seen a clip of that fantastic dunk, go to YouTube and type 'Vince Carter Frederic Weis.' Watch it and you'll see what I mean.

I've also seen some ballers destroy backboards (the rectangular-shaped board of a basketball hoop) because of their sheer size and strength. Two behemoths quickly come to mind: Darryl Dawkins and Shaquille O'Neal.

Dawkins shattered not one, but two NBA backboards after dunking in the late 1970s. The man nicknamed "Chocolate Thunder" did it twice in three weeks against the Kansas City Kings (now known as the Sacramento Kings) and San Antonio Spurs during the 1979-80 NBA season. Dawkins reared back and dunked the ball with two hands with such ferocity, he shattered the backboards to pieces.

Players had to take cover and protect themselves from shards of glass flying in all directions. Both games were delayed for at least an hour because the game crew had to fix the backboard so the game could resume.

Shaquille O'Neal followed suit almost two decades later. O'Neal broke his first backboard during his college days with the LSU Tigers in the early 1990s. It was inevitable he continued the tradition in the professional ranks because his strength was off the charts.

O'Neal damaged his first NBA hoop when he played for the Orlando Magic in the early 1990s. In a road game against Charles Barkley's Phoenix Suns, the Magic's Anthony Bowie shot a floater (a shot a player attempts while running) near the basket. O'Neal caught Bowie's shot after it bounced off the rim in mid-air, then dunked the ball in one swift motion. Although O'Neal didn't shatter the backboard, he shook the hoop's mechanism violently until the ten-foot support pole collapsed to the ground.

O'Neal struck again in a game against the New Jersey Nets (now known as the Brooklyn Nets) on April 23, 1993. O'Neal caught a pass from Donald Royal along the baseline. Since the Nets' defense converged on Royal, they were late in defending Shaq. O'Neal bounced the ball once and dunked the ball with New Jersey's Dwayne Schintzius draped all over him. He shattered the backboard and hung on to the rim to prevent himself from getting injured. That dunk was the perfect example of the so-called "Shaq Attack."

How did the slam dunk become a part of basketball? Here's a timeline of the slam dunk, a shot that traces its origins to the mid-1930s:

IN THE GAME

SLAM DUNK TIMELINE

- **1936**: Joe Fortenberry and Willard Schmidt became the first known dunkers since Dr. James Naismith invented basketball forty-five years earlier. Fortenberry and Schmidt, who played for the McPherson Globe Refiners, dunked the ball at Madison Square Garden in 1936.

- **Mid-1940s to early 1950s**: Bob Kurland was the first player who dunked regularly in games for the Phillips 66ers, a Phillips Petroleum A.A.U. basketball team. The 7'2" Kurland suited up for the 66ers for six seasons from 1946 to 1952. Unfortunately, players of that era didn't like it when opponents dunked on them – they ran under the dunker's legs in an attempt to thwart his shot.

- **1960s and 1970s**: More players such as Wilt Chamberlain, Bill Russell, "Jumping" Johnny Green, Elgin Baylor, Gus Johnson, Connie Hawkins, David Thompson, and Julius "Dr. J" Erving included the slam dunk as part of their offensive arsenals. Johnson, who suited up for the Baltimore Bullets, became the first known player to shatter an NBA backboard. Not only that, but he also did it three times within a ten-year span in the 1960s and 1970s.

The slam dunk has become a regular part of numerous NBA highlights since Chamberlain's era. However, the high school and college basketball ranks disallowed dunking from 1967 to 1978. Basketball historians traced the so-called "Lew Alcindor (Kareem Abdul-Jabbar's former name) Rule" to Alcindor's dominance with the UCLA Bruins during his college days.

The slam dunk continued its evolution in the NBA ranks. While the NBA's high school and college counterparts banned dunking in the mid-1970s, professional basketball developed breakaway rims that allowed the rim to return to its original position after a player dunks the ball.

The innovation coincided with the 1976 ABA All-Star Slam Dunk Contest – the first in professional basketball history – in Denver, CO. The final round came down to Thompson and Erving – the two most exciting dunkers of the 1970s. Erving saved his best for last. His sensational dunk from the free-throw line clinched the slam dunk title.

The NBA held its first slam dunk contest in its 1976-77 season. The participants included Kareem Abdul-Jabbar, Alex English, George Gervin, Julius Erving, Elvin Hayes, Moses Malone, and David Thompson. They competed one-on-one in various NBA arenas. Darnell "Dr. Dunk" Hillman beat Larry McNeill in the final round on June 5, 1977. Hillman received a $15,000 check for his efforts.

The NBA held its first traditional Slam Dunk Contest in Denver, CO, in 1984. Instead of players competing against one another one-on-one, they competed against the total number of participants over several rounds until the judges declared a winner. Phoenix Suns forward Larry Nance, who wowed the crowd and judges by dunking two balls in quick succession with both hands, became the 1984 NBA Slam Dunk Champion. Philadelphia 76ers guard Mac McClung, who won the event in February 2023, is the most recent winner.

Let's now break down the different types of slam dunks:

- **Tomahawk dunk:** This dunk resembles a tomahawk's chopping motion. Players typically rear back and hold the ball with one hand with the side of their bodies facing the basket. Although ballers also execute a two-handed tomahawk dunk, the one-handed version is more common.
- **Windmill dunk:** As the term implies, the dunking motion resembles a windmill. Players cradle the ball with two hands in front of their chest, execute a windmill-like motion, and throw it down with power. Ballers typically do windmill dunks on fastbreak plays when their opponents are running late on defense.
- **Double-clutch dunk:** In this type of dunk, players hold the ball in front of their chests, bring it down to their waists, and finally up to chest level again before dunking. A player can execute this dunk in a half-court set or fastbreak play depending on his athletic prowess.

- **Between-the-legs dunk:** This is one of the most difficult dunks to execute because of the athleticism and timing involved. In this situation, a player switches the ball from one hand to the other between his legs in mid-air. He dunks the ball at the end of that swift motion. The Toronto Raptors' Vince Carter made this dunk famous when he won the 2000 NBA Slam Dunk Contest in Oakland, CA.
- **Elbow-hang dunk:** When executing an elbow-hang dunk, a player typically beings with a tomahawk dunk motion. Instead of letting go of the rim after dunking the ball, the player throws his entire forearm into the hoop so he can hang on the basket with his bent elbow.
- **Alley-oop dunk:** This is a two-phase dunk that involves the 'alley' and the 'oop.' In the 'alley' phase, a player passes the basketball to his teammate. Next, the teammate who catches the ball in mid-air dunks the basketball. This is the 'oop' phase. One of the most exciting alley-oop combos in NBA history was the Seattle SuperSonics' Gary "The Glove" Payton and Shawn "The Reign Man" Kemp.
- **Reverse dunk**: In this instance, a player dunks with his back facing the basket. The dunking motion begins with the ball facing the player's chest and ends with the ball facing his nape.
- **360-degree dunk**: When a player executes a 360 dunk, he holds the ball until his body completes a 360-degree motion in mid-air. He then dunks the basketball at the end of the 360-degree movement. The Indiana Pacers' Paul George made one of the most memorable 360-degree dunks in a game against the Los Angeles Clippers in January 2014.

Let's check out five of the best slam dunkers in NBA history:
- **Julius Erving:** The man nicknamed "Dr. J" was way ahead of his time. His famous dunk from the free-throw line that clinched the 1976 ABA All-Star Game Slam Dunk Contest was hard evidence. Nobody had that kind of dunk in their arsenal back in the day. Erving's insane breakaway dunk over Michael Cooper in the 1983 NBA Finals

was one of the best in league history. The way Dr. J cradled the basketball before throwing it down over a hapless Cooper made The Spectrum (the Philadelphia 76ers' home arena) erupt in unison.

- **Dominique Wilkins:** There's a reason Wilkins earned the moniker "The Human Highlight Film" – ESPN's SportsCenter and other sports media outlets made his insane dunks part of their nightly highlight reels. Wilkins was arguably the best putback (a term for scoring a basket on a teammate's miss) dunker in league history. Wilkins, the Atlanta Hawks' two-time NBA Slam Dunk Contest champion, leaped in the air before anybody else, caught the ball, and threw it down with authority. Wilkins' repertoire also included the tomahawk and windmill dunks.

- **Michael Jordan:** Jordan could do it all: score, defend, provide leadership, and more besides. Jordan was also a showman who won two NBA Slam Dunk Contests in his legendary professional basketball career. MJ's memorable dunk from the free-throw line in the 1988 NBA Slam Dunk Contest at Chicago Stadium brought back memories of Dr. J throwing it down in the same manner in the 1976 ABA All-Star Game twelve years earlier.

- **Shawn Kemp:** Kemp was arguably the most feared dunker of the early-to-mid 1990s NBA. His rare combination of timing, athleticism, and power produced some of the most memorable dunks in NBA history. Perhaps Kemp's most memorable dunk was his insane tomahawk dunk over the Golden State Warriors' Victor Alexander in 1992. Kemp threw it down with so much force, Alexander fell on his back. A pumped-up Kemp promptly made a pointing gesture at Alexander as if to say, "In your face." Surprisingly, Shawn never won a single NBA Slam Dunk Contest in his NBA career.

- **Vince Carter**: The man known as "Vinsanity" took the NBA by storm in 1998. Carter was a popular high-flying guard who played for the North Carolina Tar Heels in college. Vince already had a penchant for throwing down vicious dunks even back then.

It wasn't any different when Carter turned pro in the fall of 1998. One of Vince's most famous dunks was his two-handed double-clutch reverse baseline dunk against the Indiana Pacers in his rookie year. Fast forward several months later in a game against the Los Angeles Clippers, Carter scored on an incredible alley-oop tomahawk dunk in transition that left Clippers center Michael Olowakandi in awe. Many basketball fans also watch Carter's immortal dunk over France's Frederic Weis in the 2000 Sydney Olympics on YouTube to this day.

I think the slam dunk is the most exciting shot in basketball. In my opinion, Vince Carter was one of the best dunkers in NBA history – even better than LeBron James and Kobe Bryant in that regard. But you need a well-rounded team, including players who can make long, high shots, like the legendary 'Skyhook' shot of Kareem Abdul-Jabbar, who we'll discuss in the next chapter.

Chapter 20:
ALL ABOUT KAREEM

It's hard to find a better basketball career than Kareem Abdul-Jabbar's. From high school to college to a storied twenty-year tenure in the NBA, he was a dominant force at all levels.

He won multiple state titles, three NCAA titles, was a six-time NBA champion, and is the only NBA player to win six Most Valuable Player Awards.

He was born Ferdinand Lewis Alcindor Jr. on April 16, 1947, in New York City. His height shot above that of his peers in adolescence and, by high school, the combination of size and skills made Lew Alcindor a devastating force at Power Memorial Academy in Manhattan.

It was at Power where he developed the skyhook, the shot that would forever define him. His head coach, Jack Donohue, encouraged him to incorporate it. Alcindor quickly rose to prominence as a basketball prodigy, leading the team to a 71-game win streak, three New York City Catholic championships, and establishing himself as one of the most dominant high school players in the country – with 2,067 points and 2,002 rebounds.

Alcindor's success at Power made him arguably the most sought after recruit – before or since. He was the biggest basketball star in New York, including anyone on the New York Knicks, or even anyone at St. John's University. So it made sense for St. John's to heavily pursue him.

IN THE GAME

He visited UCLA in April 1965, a month before his ultimate decision. He enjoyed the campus, the sunshine, the new Pauley Pavilion, and the Bruins' head coach, John Wooden.

On May 4, he chose UCLA.

Since first-year players were not allowed on varsity, Alcindor was on the Bruins freshman squad. Lew was so dominant, even in college, that his freshman club regularly defeated the main team in scrimmages.

When he became a sophomore, UCLA ignited a dynasty, winning three consecutive NCAA championships from 1967 to 1969. Alcindor was utterly dominant, and perhaps the greatest college basketball player ever, given his recognitions as a three-time National Player of the Year and a three-time Final Four Most Outstanding Player.

So dominant was Alcindor that his presence revolutionized the game of college basketball. The NCAA banned dunking from 1967 to 1976 in great part due to his indomitability in the paint.

Fortunately, Lew still had the skyhook. The patented shot, which became his trademark, involves shooting the ball with one hand, typically close to the basket, by extending the shooting arm high above the defender and releasing the ball with a sweeping motion.

Exceptional footwork and timing made it extremely difficult for defenders to block or contest the shot. His mastery of it contributed significantly to his status as a perennial top scorer.

His NBA journey began in Milwaukee. The fortunate winners of a special drawing, the Bucks got the top pick and naturally chose the former UCLA center.

Alcindor instantly made an impact in the professional ranks. He averaged 28.8 points, 14.5 rebounds, and 4.1 assists per game. Alcindor's dominance on both ends of the court earned him the NBA Rookie of the Year award – already one of the best players in the league.

The next season, both Alcindor and the Bucks would emerge as the NBA's best.

Thanks both to Alcindor and to the Bucks' 1970 acquisition of Oscar Robertson, Milwaukee finished 66-16 in the regular season, setting a record for the best single-season improvement in league history. In the playoffs, the Bucks defeated the San Francisco Warriors in the Western Conference Finals and the Baltimore Bullets in a four-game sweep to capture the franchise's first title. Alcindor was named Finals MVP, averaging 27 points and 18.5 rebounds per contest.

Later in 1971, Alcindor – who had already converted to Islam – officially changed his name to Kareem Abdul-Jabbar.

Over the years, he has spoken openly about how his faith has influenced his worldview, values, and actions both on and off the basketball court. He has been an advocate for religious tolerance and understanding, using his platform to promote peace and social justice. Abdul-Jabbar has remained an active member of the Muslim community, and has spoken about the positive impact his faith has had on his life.

That's just one of the ways Kareem has been a large off-the-court figure, too. During and after his career, he has used his platform to advocate for civil rights and social justice causes.

By 1975, Abdul-Jabbar was a perennial All-Star and MVP candidate. The Bucks had made another Finals appearance in 1974, yet their star player wanted a change of scenery. He got his wish.

In June 1975, the Los Angeles Lakers acquired Abdul-Jabbar, along with Walt Wesley, in exchange for Elmore Smith, Brian Winters, Junior Bridgeman, and Dave Meyers.

The trade had a profound impact on both franchises. Abdul-Jabbar quickly became the centerpiece of the Lakers' roster, and his arrival significantly boosted the team's profile as competitors for years to come.

For the Bucks, losing Abdul-Jabbar was the end of an era, and they struggled to replicate the success they had enjoyed with him there.

Abdul-Jabbar's pursuit to win a title in Los Angeles came up short in 1977, as the Lakers fell in the Western Conference Finals to the eventual champion

IN THE GAME

Portland Trail Blazers.

As Kareem struggled to get back to the top of the NBA, he also found difficulty garnering popularity around the nation. He came off as aloof, distant, and relatively silent. Many of those feelings were dispelled when he made a memorable cameo in the comedy film, 'Airplane.'

On the court, the insertion of Magic Johnson in 1979-80 invigorated the Lakers. That year, they won the title. And although Kareem was injured prior to the clinching game and Magic was the series hero in Game 6, Abdul-Jabbar was the unquestioned best player, and MVP of the league.

The combined forces made the Lakers into the finest team of the '80s. Kareem adapted well to the 'Showtime' fast-break style as Los Angeles won four more titles in the decade. But 1985 was Abdul-Jabbar's most satisfying triumph.

After a dreadful performance in Game 1 of the Finals in Boston, the thirty-eight-year-old rallied to put up 30 points, 17 rebounds, eight assists, and three steals in Game 2. After the teams split the next two games, Abdul-Jabbar netted 36 in the crucial Game 5. Los Angeles closed out the series with a 111-100 victory in Boston Garden, where it had lost in eight previous Finals matchups.

He was voted the NBA Finals MVP, the oldest player in history to win the honor.

Kareem retired four seasons later, capping off a twenty-year career that saw him become the NBA's all-time leading scorer with 38,387 points – a record that stood until February 7, 2023, when LeBron James surpassed it in a Lakers uniform. Abdul-Jabbar was in attendance and happily passed the torch.

Kareem Abdul-Jabbar's post-retirement career has been active as well. He has been an author, speaker, coach, and philanthropist. He has written about himself, race, religion, and social justice. He is an outspoken advocate for various social and political causes, including civil rights, racial equality, and religious tolerance. Kareem is still a large presence in our world – figuratively and literally.

Jabbar's legacy casts a big shadow across time and across America, stretching from his Harlem birth to his years of success on the opposite coast, in California. Be that as it may, there is another basketball sensation with a name which is perhaps even more universally synonymous with the place he was born, and which has a similarly large-looming legacy: The Harlem Globetrotters.

Chapter 21:
THE SHOW GOES ON: HARLEM GLOBETROTTERS

In the early twentieth century, basketball was predominantly a white sport. However, the Harlem Globetrotters changed that by becoming the first all-black basketball team to gain national and international recognition. With their feisty style of play, comedic routines, and integration of music and dance, the Globetrotters revolutionized the game and captivated audiences around the world. Join me as we explore the history and legacy of this iconic team.

Sports entrepreneur Abe Saperstein founded the Original Harlem Globetrotters in 1926. Although the team had nothing to do with Harlem (the upper East Side of Manhattan), he decided to include it in the team's name because it consisted of black basketball players. Harlem was the epicenter of African-American culture in the 1920s.

Since the Globetrotters barnstormed in predominantly white cities and towns, Saperstein wanted to give the crowds the notion his team featured African-Americans. One such town was Hinckley, IL, where the Globetrotters (who were known as the "New York Globetrotters" at the time) played their first road game on January 7, 1927.

As the Globetrotters became more popular in the years leading up to World War II, they beat the Chicago Bruins and consequently won their first World Basketball Championship in 1940. When Reece "Goose" Tatum joined the Globetrotters in 1941, they incorporated more comedic routines into their performances. Aside from the Globetrotters' remarkable juggling, trick shots, and slick passes, their hilarious punchlines made for some unique basketball comedy through the years.

Almost a decade after the Globetrotters beat the Bruins, the former proved they weren't a fluke. They beat George Mikan's Minneapolis Lakers, the defending world champions, in 1948 and 1949. The all-black team showed everybody they were the world's best. Not only that, but they also proved African-American athletes can perform beyond expectations on a global stage.

It turned out the Globetrotters' wins over the Lakers became a pivotal turning point in National Basketball Association (NBA) history. The Globetrotters' own Nat "Sweetwater" Clifton became the first black player to sign an NBA contract when he made the New York Knicks' roster in 1950. The Globetrotters also embarked on their first international tour that year.

The team took the world by storm in subsequent years. They played before 75,000 spectators at Olympic Stadium in Berlin, Germany one year after Clifton made it to the NBA. It was a remarkable feat considering basketball was still gaining popularity overseas in the early 1950s. As the years went by, it became obvious the Globetrotters weren't merely basketball players – they were global ambassadors.

In fact, the U.S. State Department wrote a letter to Globetrotters founder Abe Saperstein in 1951 that labeled them "ambassadors of extraordinary goodwill." That moniker gained traction over the years. The Globetrotters eventually earned plaudits from other global leaders such as Dwight Eisenhower and Gerald Ford as they continued barnstorming in the United States and other countries.

Before long, the Globetrotters asked former Baltimore Bullets point guard Louis "Red" Klotz to organize a team that served as their opponents during their global tours. Klotz eventually formed the Washington Generals, a team the Globetrotters typically beat when they barnstormed the United States and various countries.

The Globetrotters recruited one of the biggest names in college basketball of the late 1950s – Wilt Chamberlain. He signed with the team and played a full season for them from 1958 to 1959. The 7'1" Chamberlain eventually broke the NBA's individual game scoring record when he scored 102 points on March 2, 1962. To nobody's surprise, he became a four-time NBA MVP, seven-time All-NBA First-Team, and thirteen-time NBA All-Star in his legendary fifteen-year NBA career.

Although Chamberlain spent his best years in the NBA with the Philadelphia Warriors (now known as the Golden State Warriors) and Los Angeles Lakers, part of him was a Globetrotter through and through – he played several NBA off-seasons (the time of year between June and October when the NBA takes a four-month break) with the team during his pro basketball career.

The Harlem Globetrotters spearheaded another innovation as the basketball world ushered in the 1970s: they had their own weekly cartoon show on CBS. It was so popular, it earned rave reviews from critics and fans alike. It was one of the most popular Saturday morning cartoons of the early 1970s.

The Globetrotters made headlines in 1985 when they welcomed Lynette Woodard to their team. The Olympic gold medalist became the first female athlete who made a men's professional basketball roster. Ex-Globetrotters baller Mannie Jackson became the Globetrotters' majority owner and the first African-American sports owner eight years after Woodard suited up for the team.

Jackson was a capable owner who tripled the team's revenue in a three-year span. By the time Jackson was in his fifth year at the helm, he had quadrupled the Globetrotters' annual revenue. With Jackson leading the way, the team also contributed more than $11 million to charity.

The Harlem Globetrotters received the ultimate honor when the Naismith

Memorial Basketball Hall of Fame in Springfield, MA, inducted them in 2002 – the only team that has ever earned that elusive distinction. The team was in its seventy-sixth year of operations at the time of its induction.

The family-owned theme park company Herschend Family Entertainment purchased the team in the fall of 2013. Consequently, the company ventured into other markets at the time of the purchase.

The Harlem Globetrotters have continued to make a tremendous impact on the world since their inception in 1926. As the squad is nearing its centennial anniversary, it plays more than four hundred games in at least twenty-five countries every year.

As of this writing, almost seven hundred fifty men and women have worn the famous blue, red, and white colors of the Harlem Globetrotters. These talented basketball entertainers have performed for more than 148 million people (including famous popes, presidents, and monarchs) in 123 countries and territories around the globe for the past ninety-seven years.

The Globetrotters continue giving back to the community. The famous "Ambassadors of Goodwill" collaborate with various corporations, produce various licensed products, and spearhead numerous community projects that reach out to the less fortunate.

The Harlem Globetrotters created their Legends Ring – a group of legendary retired Globetrotters who made major contributions to the team – in 1993.

Here are ten interesting facts about the Harlem Globetrotters:

HARLEM GLOBETROTTERS

- Although the Globetrotters carry "Harlem" in their team name, they were born in the South Side of Chicago, IL, in 1926.
- The Globetrotters never played a game in Harlem, NY until 1968. They were in their forty-second year of existence when that happened.
- Chuck Cooper and Earl Lloyd – two of the first African-Americans to play in the National Basketball Association (NBA) – had brief

IN THE GAME

- stints with the Harlem Globetrotters.
- Hall of Famer Wilt Chamberlain once said his one-season stint with the Harlem Globetrotters in the late 1950s was the most fun he ever had playing professional basketball. He reportedly earned $50,000 (a large amount back in the 1950s) with the Globetrotters.
- Three eventual members of the Baseball Hall of Fame in Cooperstown, NY played for the Globetrotters: Bob Gibson, Ferguson Jenkins, and Lou Brock.
- The Washington Generals finally beat the Globetrotters thanks to a last-second shot from its player-coach, Red Klotz, on January 5, 1971. Prior to the memorable win, the Generals hadn't beaten the Globetrotters in eighteen years.
- A one-armed player named Boid Buie played for the Harlem Globetrotters from 1946 to 1955. He lost his left arm in a car accident during his teenage years.
- The Globetrotters were featured in two films in the 1950s: a self-titled 1951 feature film and *Go, Man, Go!* – a 1954 film that featured Dane Clark and Sidney Poitier. They earned a star on the Hollywood Walk of Fame in 1982.
- Jonte "Too Tall" Jones, who stood just 5'2", was the shortest player who ever played for the Globetrotters.
- On the other hand, 7'8" Paul "Tiny" Sturgess was the tallest player who ever donned Globetrotters red, blue, and white.

The Harlem Globetrotters revolutionized basketball when they came into existence in the mid-1920s. They have proven that basketball entertains millions of people and transcends boundaries around the globe for the past ninety-seven years. However, in the bigger scheme of things, basketball isn't just about sports and entertainment – it's a platform that transforms lives for the better. We will delve deeper into that aspect in the next chapter.

Chapter 22:
HOW BASKETBALL CHANGES LIVES

"But sports carried me away from being in a gang or being associated with drugs – it transforms people." – LeBron James

LeBron James: The Greatest of All-Time?

LeBron James is arguably the greatest player of his generation – the man has won four NBA MVPs and four NBA titles with three different teams. James also overtook Kareem Abdul-Jabbar as the NBA's leading scorer during the 2022-23 NBA season. As of this writing, King James has 38,652 career points entering his twenty-first year in professional basketball. It's a sure thing he will surpass 40,000 career points.

James is correct: sports transforms people. He spent his childhood in a crime-infested and seedy part of Akron, Ohio. He could've abused drugs or hung out with the wrong crowd in his youth. Instead, he used basketball as a platform for greatness. He became the best high school player in the nation in the early 2000s and eventually took the NBA by storm in the fall of 2003. James, the most popular player in the NBA, has been the epitome of greatness since then.

LeBron is just one of many ballers whose lives have been transformed by basketball. If they had chosen a different path, we never would've seen them reach their full potential on the court. Worse, we would've seen them make headlines for the wrong reasons.

Remarkably, LeBron James became a basketball icon without a reliable father figure. His father, Anthony McLelland, had many run-ins with the law. He was also never involved in young LeBron's life.

LeBron's mother Gloria James made a pivotal and life-changing decision when her son turned nine years old in 1993: she gave him her blessing to move in with local youth football coach Frank Walker. The rest, as they say, is history.

Walker introduced LeBron to basketball the year he moved in with him. It turned out the youngster was born to play the sport. Before long, eleven-year-old LeBron played organized basketball for the Amateur Athletic Union's (AAU) Northeast Ohio Shooting Stars.

James eventually starred for the St. Vincent-St. Mary Fighting Irish during his high school days. LeBron not only averaged almost thirty points per game, but he also did a little bit of everything on the basketball court: rebound, pass, and defend. It became obvious he was a man among boys – his talent level was miles ahead of his contemporaries. He eventually decided to forego his college eligibility to declare for the 2003 NBA Draft. In hindsight, it was a great decision, because he was already ripe for the NBA at a young age.

Fast forward twenty years, and LeBron James has become the NBA's biggest icon since Michael Jordan. Bear in mind LeBron is more – much more – than his awards, basketball-related accolades, and countless endorsements. LBJ (LeBron's nickname) is a known philanthropist who has given back to the community. He has his own charitable foundation, the LeBron James Family Foundation. He has also supported the After-School All-Stars, Boys & Girls Clubs of America, and Children's Defense Fund. James has also collaborated with the University of Akron – he and the school provide college scholarships to thousands of deserving students.

None of these would've been possible had LeBron James not played basketball. The timely intervention of his mother and Coach Frank Walker paved the way for the evolution of one of the NBA's greatest players of all-time.

Jeremy Lin: Mr. Linsanity

For his part, Jeremy Lin could've excelled in the corporate world after graduating from prestigious Harvard University in Cambridge, Massachusetts in 2010. However, he followed his heart and pursued basketball.

Lin, a Taiwanese-American, excelled as a high school basketball player for the Palo Alto Vikings in the mid-2000s. Jeremy submitted DVDs of his highlights to numerous Ivy League schools so he could get a basketball or academic scholarship.

Unfortunately, some coaches doubted he would excel in the collegiate ranks. Harvard Crimson assistant basketball coach Bill Holden thought Lin's ceiling was at the NCAA Division III level. Fortunately, Holden changed his mind after watching Lin play in a few scrimmage games. When Stanford University – which was just a stone's throw away from his high school – failed to offer Jeremy a scholarship, Harvard pounced on the opportunity.

Although Jeremy had a slow start with the Crimson, he eventually improved with each passing season. He averaged 17.8 points per game as a junior in the 2008 NCAA season and served notice he was a legitimate NBA prospect.

Unfortunately, no team selected Jeremy in the 2010 NBA Draft. To his surprise, Dallas Mavericks general manager Donnie Nelson invited him to mini-camp and play for their NBA Summer League team. Jeremy made the most of his opportunity and exceeded expectations. He played so well in the 2010 NBA Summer League that the Golden State Warriors, Los Angeles Lakers, and an anonymous Eastern Conference Team dangled several offers before him.

Lin decided to sign a two-year deal with his hometown Golden State Warriors prior to the 2010-11 NBA season. He eventually caught everybody's attention with his exciting style of play with the New York Knicks one season later. Jeremy was a dazzling playmaker whose forays to the basket made him a crowd favorite at Madison Square Garden in the 2011-12 NBA season. He averaged 14.6 points, 3.1 rebounds, and 6.2 assists for the Knicks that year.

Jeremy eventually played for six more teams in the next seven seasons. He never averaged fewer than 10.7 points from 2011 to 2019. He eventually earned a championship ring with the Toronto Raptors in 2019. The man nicknamed "Linsanity" proved he could excel in the NBA ranks after all.

Lin's resilience helped him overcome adversity in basketball. He didn't let his undrafted status deter him from pursuing an NBA career. Plus, he also overcame racial issues during his basketball career. He silenced the naysayers and proved that Asians can excel in basketball's biggest stage.

Kevin Durant: Simply known as "KD"

2014 NBA MVP Kevin Durant relied on basketball to overcome poverty as a child in his hometown of Washington, D.C. KD (Durant's nickname) and LeBron James have similar backgrounds: neither of their fathers played significant roles in their early lives. Think about that for a minute – two future NBA MVPs overcame fatherless childhoods to reach the top of their profession. These two ballers are survivors in every sense of the word. Fortunately for Durant, his dad Wayne Pratt made up for his absence when he accompanied Kevin to various basketball tournaments in high school.

KD wanted to become a basketball player during his formative years in the nation's capital. Ironically, he never followed his hometown Washington Wizards. Instead, he idolized Mr. "Air Canada" – the Toronto Raptors' Vince Carter.

Kevin also had the same Athletic Amateur Union (AAU) roots as LeBron James. The former suited up for AAU teams in Maryland together with future NBA players Ty Lawson, Greivis Vasquez, and Michael Beasley in the early 2000s.

Durant was already 6'0" when he was in middle school, easily towering over other kids his age. It was a sign of things to come on the basketball court. Durant played for three teams during his high school career. By the time he suited up for Montrose Christian School in 2005, he had grown to 6'7". He was just three inches short of his playing height in the National Basketball Association.

Just like LBJ, KD was a man among boys prior to playing in the NBA. The latter averaged an impressive 25.8 points per game and earned Consensus First-Team All-American and Big 12 Player of the Year honors as true freshman forward with the Texas Longhorns in 2006.

KD decided to declare for the 2007 NBA Draft, where the then-Seattle SuperSonics (now known as the Oklahoma City Thunder) made him the second overall selection behind the Portland Trail Blazers' Greg Oden. Durant has never looked back – he has never averaged fewer than 20.3 points in a combined sixteen NBA seasons with the Seattle SuperSonics, Oklahoma City Thunder, Golden State Warriors, Brooklyn Nets, and Phoenix Suns.

Durant, one of the most feared scorers in the NBA, has earned numerous accolades, including two NBA titles with the Warriors, thirteen NBA All-Star Game appearances, and six All-NBA First-Team selections. The NBA 75th Anniversary Team member has also led the league in scoring four times.

Basketball has been kind to Kevin Durant. The game has opened many doors for him – he is an endorser of Nike, Gatorade, Sprint, Panini, General Electric, and 2K Sports; minority owner of Major League Soccer's (MLS) Philadelphia Union; and co-founder of the media company Thirty Five Ventures. KD is also an active philanthropist who has contributed to numerous charitable causes such as the American Red Cross and the non-profit organization P'Tones Records. Durant likely wouldn't have made a tremendous impact on society had it not been for basketball.

Dirk Nowitzki: The Dallas Mavericks' Mr. Clutch

On a different note, we discussed the evolution of the NBA in Chapter Four. Part of the growth involved the league's internationalization – the rise of basketball players from overseas. Several German players such as Uwe Blab and Detlef Schrempf made an impact on the NBA in the 1980s and 1990s, respectively. Although they had tremendous upsides, neither Blab nor Schrempf made a bigger impact than the Dallas Mavericks' Dirk Nowitzki.

Nowitzki was a complete unknown when he entered the NBA in 1998. The Milwaukee Bucks, who made him the ninth overall selection of the 1998 NBA Draft, traded him to the Mavericks for former Michigan Wolverines big man, Robert "Tractor" Traylor. It became one of the most one-sided trades in league history. Nowtizki became a franchise player, fourteen-time NBA All-Star, and a possible future Hall-of-Famer. On the other hand, Traylor never averaged more than 5.3 points per game in a disappointing seven-year NBA career.

Nobody predicted Nowitzki would become one of the greatest scorers of his generation. Mavericks owner Mark Cuban acknowledged that fact to CBS Sports' James Herbert in the days leading up to Dirk's retirement in the fall of 2019.

"I didn't know how good he would be," Cuban told Herbert. "Had no idea."

Dirk's NBA career took off after his second year in Dallas in 2012. He never averaged fewer than 21.6 points in thirteen of his next twenty NBA seasons. Nowitzki, a 7'0" forward-center, wasn't your typical big man who made a living in the low-post area. Instead, Dirk thrived on medium- and long-range jumpers from at least twelve feet from the basket. His patented fadeaway baseline jumper (as the term implies, it's a shot a player attempts while seemingly falling backward) was virtually unblockable. Defenders had no chance – they couldn't even lay a finger on Dirk's fadeaway.

Dirk Nowitzki, the greatest German-born NBA player of all-time, averaged 20.7 points, 7.5 rebounds, and 2.4 assists in his remarkable twenty-one-year NBA career from 1998 to 2018. The four-time All-NBA First-Team selection and NBA 75th Anniversary Team member helped the Mavericks win their first NBA championship in 2011.

Nowitzki was the perfect example of an unknown player rising from obscurity to become a basketball legend. Basketball helped him inspire many youngsters to achieve their goals no matter how impossible they may seem.

Maya Moore: A Valuable Part of the Minnesota Lynx Dynasty in the Late 2010s

On the women's basketball front, Maya Moore was a dynamic scorer for the WNBA's Minnesota Lynx from 2011 to 2018. She first played basketball when she was three years old in Jefferson City, Missouri. Fast forward thirteen years, and the sixteen-year-old Maya dunked a basketball for the first time during warm-ups while playing for her high school basketball team, the Collins Hill Eagles.

Moore became one of the greatest female basketball players the state of Georgia has ever produced. She was a three-time Georgia 5A Player of the Year who averaged 25.5 points and 12.1 rebounds as a senior in 2006. Maya eventually became one of the best players of Geno Auriemma's UConn Huskies of the late 2000s. She averaged 19.7 points and 8.3 rebounds per game in four years for the Huskies from 2007 to 2010.

Moore, a two-time *Associated Press* College Player of the Year, became one of the hottest rookie prospects of the 2011 WNBA Draft. She picked up where she left off from the collegiate ranks and averaged 18.4 points, 5.9 rebounds, and 3.3 assists in her eight-year WNBA career, all spent with the Minnesota Lynx.

The trio of Maya Moore, Seimone Augustus, and Lindsay Whalen helped the Lynx become the most dominant team of the late 2010s. With the three players firing on all cylinders, the Lynx won the WNBA title in 2011 and 2013. When perennial All-Star center Sylvia Fowles joined them in 2015, Minnesota won two more WNBA championships in 2015 and 2017.

For her part, Moore earned six WNBA All-Star, five All-WNBA First Team, and two All-WNBA selections in her stellar eight-year WNBA career. Maya is also a member of the WNBA's 20th and 25th Anniversary Teams.

IN THE GAME

Maya Moore made a profound impact on society two years after she retired from the WNBA. Thanks to her relentless efforts, she helped free convicted felon Jonathan Irons from prison in 2020; the judge overturned his wrongful conviction. Irons was serving a fifty-year prison sentence in Jefferson City, Missouri, at the time of his release. Maya took a leave of absence from the WNBA in 2019 so she could help free Irons. Moore hasn't played professional basketball since she went on leave. She and Irons got married in the summer of 2020. Their union produced a son, Jonathan Irons, Jr.

Moore proved basketball players are more than just remarkable athletes – they can make a difference in society as well. She has inspired young female ballers to excel on the court and change society for the better. Indeed, Maya Moore is a special breed of WNBA player.

As LeBron James, Jeremy Lin, Kevin Durant, Dirk Nowitzki, and Maya Moore have shown, basketball isn't just about sports and entertainment – it helps transform people from all walks of life. The sport has changed their lives forever.

These changes are present in the lives of individuals, but also basketball has proven its ability to shift whole cultures. Nowhere is that more apparent than in hip-hop, which we'll discuss in the next chapter.

Chapter 23:
IMPACT OF BASKETBALL ON HIP-HOP CULTURE

Basketball is a sport that naturally has an impact beyond the arenas, extending into many areas of society. Nowhere is this more apparent than in the influence the sport has on a particular music genre.

The influence of basketball on hip-hop culture is profound and multifaceted. The two often intersect in many ways.

Basketball fashion has a strong foothold – from apparel to celebrity endorsements. Its jerseys, consequently, have been a staple of hip-hop fashion since the early years of the genre. Artists and fans alike often feature their favorite teams or players as a form of self-expression and fandom. They are often worn as fashion statements by hip-hop artists and fans. The vibrant colors, bold designs, and iconic logos of NBA teams make jerseys stand out as stylish and eye-catching apparel.

Hip-hop artists frequently wear them to showcase their allegiance to their hometown, as embodied by the local team. Loyalty to one's roots is an evergreen theme in hip-hop, hence jerseys acknowledging an artist's place of origin can serve as visual symbols of that loyalty.

Retro and throwback jerseys have experienced a resurgence in popularity. Classic designs and logos from past eras evoke a sense of nostalgia and authenticity. Artists and fans also personalize their jerseys by adding custom designs, patches, or embroidery. This customization allows individuals to put their own unique spin on the jersey, making it a more personal and meaningful fashion statement.

Artists often collaborate with sportswear brands and teams to release limited edition jersey collections. These collaborations often feature unique designs, colorways, and graphics inspired by the artist's music, style, or cultural influence. All these jerseys – whether they are current, custom, or retro – are featured prominently in music videos and live performances for the purpose of cross-promotion.

Sneakers, particularly those endorsed by players, or iconic brands like Nike and Adidas, have become integral to hip-hop fashion. Sneaker culture is deeply intertwined with hip-hop, with artists frequently referencing and showcasing the latest sneaker releases in their music videos, lyrics, and public appearances. One need look no further for proof of the importance of basketball in these aesthetic concerns than to hear the countless lyrics dedicated to mocking people for having knockoff Air Jordan basketball shoes.

 The influence is more ubiquitous than jerseys and shoes alone, though: hoodies, sweatpants, and tracksuits reminiscent of basketball warm-up gear are commonly worn by hip-hop artists and fans.

Team logos and branding elements are often incorporated into hip-hop fashion, appearing on clothing and accessories, and even in tattoos.

Endorsement deals between players and sportswear brands mirror the same sorts of deals made between those brands and famous rappers, singers, and producers, drawing the two worlds even closer together. Artists regularly collaborate with athletes and brands on sneaker releases, apparel lines, and promotional campaigns. Many players and artists have developed close friendships and mutual admiration for each other's work. These friendships often extend beyond the court and the studio, with athletes and artists frequently attending each other's games, concerts, and events.

They collaborate on a variety of projects: music videos, commercials, and charitable initiatives. Artists may perform at halftime shows during games or make guest appearances at basketball-related events. This cross-promotion helps to bridge the worlds of sports and music, reaching broader audiences and reinforcing the connection between basketball and hip-hop.

Many artists incorporate basketball imagery into their songs, ranging from abstract metaphors to concrete stat references. Basketball terminology and player names are ripe cultural reference points for conveying themes of competition, success, determination, and street credibility.

Both basketball players and hip-hop artists wield significant influence on social media, with millions of followers eagerly consuming their content and engaging with their posts. This influence extends to fashion, lifestyle, and cultural trends, with athletes and artists shaping popular discourse and setting new standards for style and behavior.

Advocacy is another way in which basketball culture and hip-hop intersect. Many players and artists use their platforms to advocate for social justice, community empowerment, and charitable causes. They frequently collaborate on initiatives to address issues such as racial inequality, poverty, and educational disparities, leveraging their combined influence to effect positive change.

Streetball, with its emphasis on creativity, improvisation, and individual skill, shares similarities with hip-hop. Both are both forms of creative expression that originated in urban environments – with participants encouraged to express themselves creatively and experiment with new moves, techniques, and rhythms. They offer a forum in which to showcase talents, style, and personality through music, art, fashion, and basketball skills.

Local courts and hip-hop events serve as gathering places where people from diverse backgrounds come together to socialize, compete, and celebrate their shared love for basketball and music. These spaces foster a sense of community and connection among participants, creating bonds that transcend cultural, social, and economic differences.

Participants often incorporate elements of urban fashion, including baggy clothing, sneakers, and accessories, into their on-court and off-court attire, reflecting the influence of hip-hop on streetball culture and vice versa.

Hip-hop music is an integral part of the streetball experience, providing the soundtrack for games, tournaments, and outdoor courts. Players and spectators often blast hip-hop tracks from boomboxes or speakers, creating an energetic and vibrant atmosphere that enhances the overall streetball experience.

Both environments also possess spirits of healthy competition and mutual respect. While games may be intense and competitive, there is also a sense of camaraderie and sportsmanship on and off the court, with players showing respect for each other's skills, talent, and dedication.

Basketball and hip-hop have also been depicted in many well-respected films and documentaries. 'Hoop Dreams' is a legendary sports film, equally lauded by sports fans and cinephiles as one of the best of its kind. Released in 1994, it follows the lives of two black high school students, William Gates and Arthur Agee, as they try to become professional basketball players. Over the course of five years, it chronicles the challenges, triumphs, and setbacks on and off the basketball court.

'Hoop Dreams' offers a raw and intimate look at the realities of inner-city life, highlighting issues such as poverty, race, education, and the American Dream. It explores the complex intersection of sports, race, and socioeconomic status, shedding light on the systemic barriers and inequalities that shape their lives and aspirations.

The documentary was critically acclaimed and won the Academy Award for Best Film Editing.

'Through the Fire' follows the journey of Sebastian Telfair, a highly touted high school player from Coney Island, Brooklyn, and shows the intersection of hip-hop and the world of sports.

'He Got Game,' from 1998, stars Hall of Famer Ray Allen as Jesus Shuttlesworth, and Oscar winner Denzel Washington as his father. It's directed by Spike Lee, and depicts the highs and lows of a star high schooler on the road to fame. All of these films feature recognizable soundtracks with prominent use of hip-hop music (in some cases also incorporating jazz, which in the case of 'He Got Game' was used to great effect by Spike Lee as a way to highlight the generational cultural differences between father and son, in turn displaying changes in the culture of impoverished areas of New York over the decades).

Overall, basketball's influence on hip-hop culture is pervasive and enduring, shaping not only the music but also the fashion, language, and values of urban communities around the world.

Fashion isn't always just about looks, though, as we can see from how many players revere certain items of clothing as protective charms, which they feel guard them, along with the performance of superstitious rituals.

Chapter 24:
FROM LUCKY SOCKS TO SUPERSTITIONS: INSIDE THE QUIRKY WORLD OF BASKETBALL RITUALS

Have you ever wondered why some basketball players have strange rituals before games?

From wearing lucky socks to eating the same meal, these quirky superstitions have become a part of the sport's culture. Dive into the world of basketball home-court rituals and discover how these unique habits impact the game.

Let's check out some of the most interesting NBA superstitions of all-time:

Michael Jordan: Even the GOAT had his superstitious side: he always wore his North Carolina Tar Heels practice shorts underneath his regular NBA trousers. Unfortunately, his powder blue college practice shorts dangled underneath his Chicago Bulls shorts in the mid-to-late 1980s.

When longer shorts (courtesy of Michigan's 'Fab Five') became the trend in the early 1990s, Jordan followed suit and wore longer shorts. Nobody saw a glimpse of his North Carolina practice shorts until his final retirement with the Washington Wizards in 2003.

MJ had another ritual before Chicago Bulls home games: he dusted his hands with powdered rosin to help enhance his grip on the basketball. Jordan did his dusting ritual before Bulls announcer Johnny "Red" Kerr every time. When Jordan was finished, he clapped his hands in front of Kerr, whose face was smothered with rosin powder before his broadcasts. NBA superstars Kevin Garnett and LeBron James also undertook the rosin powder pre-game ritual several years later.

Kevin Garnett: KG was one of the prominent NBA superstars who dusted their hands off with powdered rosin before games. Not only that, but the fifteen-time NBA All-Star also ate a peanut butter and jelly sandwich before tip-off for twenty seasons.

LeBron James: James was another NBA superstar who always dusted his hands with powdered rosin before taking the court. LeBron also has a habit of chewing his fingernails while he's sitting on the bench.

James wore a headband in his first twelve NBA seasons from 2003 to 2014. However, he decided not to wear a headband anymore beginning the 2014-15 NBA season as a sign of unity with his teammates.

"I did it because I just wanted to look like my teammates," James told *The Northeast Ohio Media Group* (via CBS Sports' Matt Moore) in the spring of 2015. "Just wanted to be one. Nothing more than that."

LeBron was in his second stint with his hometown Cleveland Cavaliers at the time. He helped the Cavs win their first NBA title a year-and-a-half after ditching his famous headband.

Caron Butler: NBA journeyman (a player who suited up for many teams during his basketball career) Caron Butler guzzled a two-liter bottle of Mountain Dew in the first few years of his fourteen-season NBA career. He drank half of the bottle before the game and finished off the contents at halftime. According to SI.com, Butler started doing that ritual during his high school days in his hometown of Racine, Wisconsin.

Butler played for the Washington Wizards from 2005 to 2009. It was during this four-year time frame when the Wizards asked him to stop drinking Mountain Dew before and during games. Butler eventually obliged.

Caron also had a unique way of dealing with his nervous energy on game days: he chewed on straws. He told ESPN (via SI.com) he usually cut several pieces of black McDonald's or Burger King straws and chewed on them while he was sitting on the bench. The NBA has since outlawed that unusual habit.

Mark Jackson: Jackson, a flashy, Brooklyn-born point guard, played for the New York Knicks, Los Angeles Clippers, Indiana Pacers, Toronto Raptors, Utah Jazz, and Houston Rockets in his eighteen-season NBA career. Mark always tied his wedding ring to his shoelace in every game after he got married in the summer of 1990.

Ray Allen: Before guys such as Stephen Curry, Klay Thompson, and Damian Lillard took the court, Ray Allen was the premiere shooter of his era. One of the secrets to his success lay in his consistency. Ray never wavered from this daily routine:

- Take a nap from 11:30 a.m. to 1 p.m.
- Consume a pre-game meal that included chicken and rice at 2:30 p.m.
- Shave head and then go to the arena at 3:30 p.m.
- Shoot warm-up shots three hours before tip-off

Rajon Rondo: The controversial point guard is known for his playmaking abilities and nifty passes. However, many fans don't know he takes *five* showers on days when his team is playing.

Tim Duncan: Duncan, a five-time NBA champion, two-time NBA MVP, and fifteen-time NBA All-Star, was one of the most superstitious ballers of his era. One of his pre-game rituals had him hanging on the rim before the stadium announcer introduced him before games.

Duncan had another interesting superstition: he always wore his practice shorts *backwards*. He told an anonymous reporter (via SI.com) he began this ritual during his college days with the Wake Forest Demon Deacons in the mid-1990s:

"I wear my practice shorts backwards during practice. In college, I came out of the locker room one practice and later realized my shorts were on backwards, so I didn't bother to correct them. I had a great practice, and ever since it has been a tradition for me."

Jason Terry: Michael Jordan and Tim Duncan weren't the only ones who were superstitious about wearing their shorts. Veteran point guard Jason Terry took that ritual to a different level. Terry wore the opposing team's shorts the night before he played against them. Terry collected those shorts from his inner circle: friends, equipment managers, and other NBA players.

Jason also ate chicken as part of his pre-game meal. Not only that, he also wore *five* pairs of socks whenever he played.

Dwyane Wade: Wade, a three-time NBA champion and thirteen-time NBA All-Star, hung from the rim before every game just like his contemporaries Tim Duncan, Kevin Garnett, and Vince Carter.

However, Wade didn't just hang from the rim, he hung above it: he did three pull-ups and pulled his head above the rim during pre-game introductions. There's no question the man nicknamed "D-Wade" and "Flash" redefined the term 'above the rim' during his sixteen-season NBA career from 2003 to 2018.

Bill Russell: Russell was a defensive menace whose epic showdowns with Wilt "The Stilt" Chamberlain remain among the best in NBA history. Bill earned an incredible eleven NBA championship rings and helped the Boston Celtics become the gold standard of professional basketball in the 1950s and 1960s.

Although Russell was tenacious on the basketball court, he had a soft side off it – his teammates and friends thought his boisterous laugh stood out. Russell's ritual was vomiting before and during games. His Celtics teammate John "Hondo" Havlicek recalled Bill's strange superstition (via SI.com):

"He used to throw up all the time before a game or at halftime. A tremendous sound – almost as loud as his laugh. It's a welcome sound, too.

IN THE GAME

Because it means he's keyed up for a game, and around the locker room, we grin and say, 'Man, we're going to be all right tonight.'"

Even legendary Boston Celtics head coach Red Auerbach was convinced Russell's vomiting ritual became an integral part of the team's success.

Auerbach once didn't hear Russell throw up prior to a pivotal playoff game. The former ordered his players (who were already warming up on the court) to return to the locker room. Auerbach told them to stay there until Russell vomited to his heart's content.

Jeff Hornacek: Hornacek, a sharp-shooting guard who helped the Utah Jazz reach the NBA Finals in 1997 and 1998, had an unusual free-throw shooting routine. Jeff wiped his face three times and took several dribbles before shooting. It was his way of saying hello to his children who watched his games from their house.

Jason Kidd: Kidd, an outstanding playmaker, was another player with a strange free-throw ritual. He stepped up to the free-throw line, took the ball from the referee, cradled the ball with his left hand while blowing a kiss to the rim with his right hand, took one dribble, and shot the free throw. Jason blowing a kiss to the rim was his way of expressing his love to his family who watched the game on television.

Dirk Nowtizki: Nowitzki, the greatest German player who ever played in the National Basketball Association, was another superstar who had an unusual free-throw shooting routine. Dirk felt the pressure of shooting free throws early in his illustrious twenty-season NBA career.

A coach gave him some life-changing advice: hum a song while shooting the free throw to relax. Before long, Dirk started humming the Counting Crows song 'Mr. Jones' while shooting his free throws. Apparently, the ploy worked, because Nowitzki was a career 87.9 percent free throw shooter.

Stephen Curry: Curry, Ray Allen, Reggie Miller, Klay Thompson, and Larry Bird are some of the best shooters in NBA history. One of Stephen's superstitions is wearing his trademark lavender Curry 4 Flowtrow shoes. Strangely enough, his team, the Golden State Warriors, always wins whenever Steph wears those kicks (a basketball term for shoes).

Curry wore his lavender shoes in the Warriors' series-clinching Game 4 victory over the Memphis Grizzlies in the 2022 Western Conference Finals. When Steph wore a different pair of shoes in game 3 of the 2022 NBA Finals against the Boston Celtics, the Warriors lost, 116-100. Curry decided enough was enough – he wore his Curry 4 Flowtros in Golden State's next three games. Sure enough, the Warriors beat the Celtics three straight times to clinch their seventh title in franchise history. For his part, Steph earned his fourth championship ring thanks to his lavender kicks.

Superstitions have been a part of the National Basketball Association since its inception in 1949. These rituals range from the typical pre-game meals to the unusual antics such as hanging onto the basketball rims and wearing practice shorts backwards. It just goes to show you NBA players will do anything to play at a high level and help their teams win on the game's biggest stage.

Conclusion

Basketball has come a long way since Dr. James Naismith installed two peach baskets at a YMCA in Springfield, Massachusetts on a cold, blustery day in December 1891. The game has evolved over the past 132 years. What used to be a simple team sport in the late nineteenth century has now become a cultural and global phenomenon that transcends international boundaries. Indeed, basketball isn't just a sport nowadays – it's a way of life for many hoops junkies the world over.

Who would've thought basketball – a game grown men used to play in cages – would make its debut in the 1936 Berlin Olympics when the world was on the brink of war? Despite the imminent conflict among nations, basketball gained serious traction over the years. Cagers who stood at least 6'0" relied on two-handed set shots to win low-scoring games in the 1940s. Before long, the National Basketball Association (NBA) became the world's undisputed hotbed of professional basketball.

If you've leafed through the pages of a basketball encyclopedia, photos of players such as George Mikan, Vern Mikkelsen, Bob Cousy, Bill Russell and Wilt Chamberlain depicted the prevailing fashion sense on the hardcourt during their era: body-hugging jerseys and skin-tight shorts that made you wonder if they could breathe at all during games. Chamberlain was one of the pioneers of the headband many players wear today. Not only that, but we've also seen arms sleeves, knee wraps, and jersey t-shirts become the norm among players and fans alike these days.

Guys such as Elgin Baylor, Connie "The Hawk" Hawkins, Elvin Hayes, Julius "Dr. J" Erving, David Thompson, "Pistol" Pete Maravich, John "Hondo"

Havlicek, and Mr. NBA logo himself, Jerry West, became professional basketball's torch bearers in the 1960s and 1970s. They eventually passed the torch to Earvin "Magic" Johnson and Larry Bird, whose epic rivalry in the 1980s has stood the test of time. When the Lakers vs. Celtics rivalry waned in the late 1980s, the Detroit Pistons and eventually Michael Jordan took over the reins as the NBA's best. The San Antonio Spurs, Miami Heat, and Golden State Warriors have taken turns dominating the NBA landscape in the twenty-first century.

As the NBA continues to expand its global reach, we've also seen other ballers such as Kobe Bryant and Vince Carter capture the hearts and imaginations of millions of basketball fans. Today, guys such as LeBron James, Stephen Curry, Nikola Jokic, and Kawhi Leonard – to name a few – continue to set the bar high in the modern NBA.

The ladies aren't pushovers by any stretch – the WNBA has also inspired thousands of aspiring female basketball players to achieve their dreams. We will never forget the legacy ballers such as Tamika Catchings, Cynthia Cooper, Lisa Leslie, Tina Thompson, and Sheryl Swoopes established for the younger female generation. A new breed of WNBA hoopsters such as A'ja Wilson, Sabrina Ionescu, Marina Mabrey, Brianna Stewart, Chelsea Gray, Jewel Lloyd, and Aliyah Boston carry their legacies today.

Professional basketball leagues have also taken Europe, Asia, and Australia by storm. Even if recreational players don't make it to the professional level, they showcase their skills in playgrounds and makeshift basketball courts all over the world. Basketball is now a global phenomenon.

On that note, basketball hasn't merely transcended international boundaries – it has demolished barriers and helped unite people from all walks of life. After all, basketball and sports in general have one ulterior motive: they help unite the community. When fans rally behind their favorite teams and players, they foster an unbreakable bond – that is what ultimately matters in the long run.

With that in mind, I hope this great game has taught you valuable lessons such as perseverance and resilience in your journey as a basketball fan.

IN THE GAME

Please don't hesitate to share the basketball-related stories and lessons you learned to show everybody how amazing and great this game is. Share your honest review of this book on amazon.com so you can help other people increase their basketball knowledge.

As a parting shot, I want to thank you for embarking on this epic basketball journey with me. Whether you're a new basketball fan or lifelong hoops junkie, this game will continue to touch lives and make Dr. James Naismith proud forever.

Share Your Thoughts on "In The Game: 24 Short Stories About the Extraordinary Game of Basketball"

Now that you've enjoyed the thrilling tales and inspiring moments in "In The Game," it's time to pass on the excitement. By sharing your honest opinion of "In The Game: 24 Short Stories About the Extraordinary Game of Basketball" on Amazon, you're not just reviewing a book – you're sharing the love of basketball with other fans eager to dive into the world of this incredible sport.

Your Opinion Matters
Your review is a guiding light for others, leading them to the treasure trove of stories and passion for basketball found within the pages of this book. By taking a moment to leave your thoughts, you're contributing to a community of basketball enthusiasts who inspire each other to reach new heights.

How You Can Help:
1. Scan the QR code below to leave your review on Amazon.
2. Share your experiences and insights – be the guiding force for someone else's basketball journey.

Why Your Review Matters:
- Your words help others discover the joy and excitement of basketball.
- You pass on the torch of passion for the game to fellow fans.
- Together, we keep the spirit of basketball alive by sharing our stories and knowledge.

Thank You for Your Contribution
Your commitment to enjoying the game and helping others deserves appreciation. By leaving a review, you're playing a vital role in nurturing a community of basketball fans who support each other.

Scan the QR code below to leave your review on Amazon (just so you know, this takes you to the review page of Amazon US, if you live in a different country, simply change the .com to the relevant country domain suffix. Or you can go to your order page to leave a review there):

Thank you for being part of this basketball journey and for making "In The Game" a source of inspiration for others as they explore the wonders of the game.

Gratefully,

Jamie Adler

References

ESPN. (2005, December 13). [Title of the Article]. https://www.espn.com/espn/page2/story?page=neel/051213

NBA. (2018, December 10). Unforgettable Moments: NBA's Highest Scoring Game. https://www.nba.com/watch/video/2018/12/10/unforgettable-moments-nbas-highest-scoring-game?plsrc=nba&collection=nba-history-great-regular-season-games

Gatorade Sports Science Institute. (n.d.). Game of Basketball. https://www.gssiweb.org/sports-science-exchange/article/game-of-basketball

FanSided. (2022, October 28). How Many Games in an NBA Season? https://fansided.com/2022/10/28/how-many-games-nba-season/

National Center for Biotechnology Information. (n.d.). [Title of the Article]. https://www.ncbi.nlm.nih.gov/pmc/articles/PMC6096539/

PubMed. (n.d.). [Title of the Article]. https://pubmed.ncbi.nlm.nih.gov/33673427/

Hindawi. (2022). [Title of the Article]. https://www.mdpi.com/2075-4663/10/10/139

MDPI. (2022). [Title of the Article]. https://www.mdpi.com/2075-4663/10/10/139

CoachUp. (n.d.). 10 Qualities That Make a Basketball Player Great. https://www.coachup.com/nation/articles/10-qualities-that-make-a-basketball-player-great

Select Basketball USA. (2017, May 12). Eight Traits for Success. https://

selectbasketballusa.com/blog/2017/05/12/eight-traits-for-success/

Watts Basketball. (n.d.). Qualities of a Good Basketball Player. https://wattsbasketball.com/blog/qualities-of-a-good-basketball-player

Naismith Memorial Basketball Hall of Fame. (n.d.). Our Mission & Election Process. https://www.hoophall.com/about/about-hall/our-mission/election-process/

Basketball Noise. (n.d.). What Are the Requirements for the NBA Hall of Fame? https://basketballnoise.com/what-are-the-requirements-for-the-nba-hall-of-fame/

Basketball Mindset Training. (n.d.). 24 Motivational Basketball Quotes. https://www.basketballmindsettraining.com/blog/24-motivational-basketball-quotes

NBA Lead. (n.d.). A Typical Day of an NBA Player During the Season. https://nbalead.com/typical-day-of-nba-player-during-season/

Quora. (n.d.). What's a Day in the Life Like During the Season for an NBA Player? https://www.quora.com/Whats-a-day-in-the-life-like-during-the-season-for-an-NBA-player

ESPN. (n.d.). NBA All-Time Leaders. http://www.espn.com/nba/history/leaders

Inquirer.net. (n.d.). NBA: Ja Morant Suspended by Grizzlies After New Video with Gun. https://sports.inquirer.net/510317/nba-ja-morant-suspended-by-grizzlies-suspend-after-new-video-with-gun

Boston.com. (2023, April 11). Paul Pierce Fired by ESPN: Background and 2021 Incident. https://www.boston.com/sports/morning-sports-update/2023/04/11/paul-pierce-espn-fired-background-2021/

Black EOE Journal. (2019, January). LeBron James: Five Humongous Charitable Donations. https://blackeoejournal.com/2019/01/lebron-james-five-humongous-charitable-donations/

Basha Bears Basketball. (n.d.). LeBron James: A True Champion of Charity and Generosity. https://bashabearsbasketball.com/lebron-james-a-true-champion-of-charity-and-generosity/

Hoop Maestro. (n.d.). The Most Charitable NBA Players. https://hoopmaestro.com/the-most-charitable-nba-players/

Bleacher Report. (n.d.). 10 NBA Players with the Most Love for Their Communities. https://bleacherreport.com/articles/1992200-10-nba-players-with-the-most-love-for-their-communities

ClutchPoints. (n.d.). Dennis Rodman: Most Controversial Moments. https://clutchpoints.com/dennis-rodman-most-controversial-moments

Sports Management Degrees. (n.d.). Five Most Controversial Players in NBA History. https://www.sports-management-degrees.com/lists/five-most-controversial-players-in-nba-history/

BrainyQuote. (n.d.). James Naismith Quotes. https://www.brainyquote.com/authors/james-naismith-quotes

Wikipedia. (n.d.). History of Basketball. https://en.wikipedia.org/wiki/History_of_basketball

Jr. NBA. (n.d.). James Naismith: Invention of Basketball. https://jr.nba.com/james-naismith-invention-basketball/

Wonderopolis. (n.d.). Who Invented Basketball? https://wonderopolis.org/wonder/who-invented-basketball

Hoop Heads Pod. (n.d.). A Brief History of Basketball. https://hoopheadspod.com/a-brief-history-of-basketball/

History.com. (n.d.). How a Canadian Invented Basketball. https://www.history.com/news/how-a-canadian-invented-basketballm

Dunk or Three. (n.d.). Why Are Basketball Players Called Cagers? https://dunkorthree.com/why-basketball-players-called-cagers/

Daily Press. (1999, August 25). Basketball Once Was Played in a Wire Cage. https://www.dailypress.com/1999/08/25/basketball-once-was-played-in-a-wire-cage/

Rookie Road. (n.d.). Basketball Cagers. https://www.rookieroad.com/basketball/terms/cagers/

Dunk or Three. (n.d.). Why Are Basketball Players Called Cagers? https://

dunkorthree.com/why-basketball-players-called-cagers/

Sportskeeda. (n.d.). Basketball Cage Matches: The Beginning and the End. https://www.sportskeeda.com/basketball/basketball-cage-matches-the-beginning-and-the-end

SI Vault. (1991, November 11). When the Court Was a Cage. https://vault.si.com/vault/1991/11/11/when-the-court-was-a-cage-in-the-early-days-of-pro-basketball-the-players-were-segregated-from-the-fans

Bleacher Report. (n.d.). The 5 Fights That Changed the NBA. https://bleacherreport.com/articles/2892788-the-5-fights-that-changed-the-nba

Bleacher Report. (n.d.). Recording of James Naismith Describes 1st Game of Basketball as an All-Out Brawl. https://bleacherreport.com/articles/2599298-recording-of-james-naismith-describes-1st-game-of-basketball-as-an-all-out-brawl

Kids Listen. (n.d.). Why Did the First Basketball Games Always End in Big Fights? https://app.kidslisten.org/ep/Who-Smarted-Why-did-the-first-basketball-games-always-end-in-big-fights

Los Angeles Times. (n.d.). James Naismith's New Recording. https://www.latimes.com/sports/sportsnow/la-sp-sn-james-naismith-new-recording-20151215-htmlstory.html

TallSome. (n.d.). Basketball Fights. https://tallsome.com/basketball-fights/

Wikipedia. (n.d.). Malice at the Palace. https://en.wikipedia.org/wiki/Malice_at_the_Palace

The Guardian. (2021, August 10). Untold Malice at the Palace: Pistons-Pacers Documentary. https://www.theguardian.com/sport/2021/aug/10/untold-malice-at-the-palace-pistons-pacers-documentary

Wikipedia. (n.d.). National Basketball Association. https://en.wikipedia.org/wiki/National_Basketball_Association

Wikipedia. (n.d.). List of NBA Players Born Outside the United States. https://en.wikipedia.org/wiki/List_of_NBA_players_born_outside_the_United_States

ClutchPoints. (n.d.). The Evolution of Foreign Players in the NBA. https://clutchpoints.com/the-evolution-of-foreign-players-in-the-nba

Wikipedia. (n.d.). National Basketball Association. https://en.wikipedia.org/wiki/National_Basketball_Association

History.com. (n.d.). NBA Is Born. https://www.history.com/this-day-in-history/nba-is-born

Britannica. (n.d.). National Basketball Association. https://www.britannica.com/topic/National-Basketball-Association

NBA Hoops Online. (n.d.). History of the NBA. https://nbahoopsonline.com/History/

NBA Careers. (n.d.). History of the NBA. https://careers.nba.com/history/

Wikipedia. (n.d.). Expansion of the National Basketball Association. https://en.wikipedia.org/wiki/Expansion_of_the_National_Basketball_Association

Naismith Memorial Basketball Hall of Fame. (n.d.). First Team. https://www.hoophall.com/hall-of-famers/first-team/

Omeka. (n.d.). Basketball Players. https://basketballplayers.omeka.net/

Englund, G. (n.d.). Gene Englund. Wikipedia. https://en.wikipedia.org/wiki/Gene_Englund

Edwards, M. (n.d.). Big Blue History: Kentucky Wildcats Basketball Page. http://www.bigbluehistory.net/bb/Edwards/index.html

Hoophall. (n.d.). Bobby McDermott. Naismith Memorial Basketball Hall of Fame. https://www.hoophall.com/hall-of-famers/bobby-mcdermott/

McDermott, B. (n.d.). Bobby McDermott. Wikipedia. https://en.wikipedia.org/wiki/Bobby_McDermott

Riebe, M. (n.d.). Mel Riebe. Wikipedia. https://en.wikipedia.org/wiki/Mel_Riebe

West, J. (n.d.). Who is Jerry West, the Inspiration for the NBA Logo? Who Designed It? AS. https://en.as.com/nba/who-is-jerry-west-the-inspiration-for-the-nba-logo-who-designed-it-n/

West, J. (n.d.). Jerry West. Wikipedia. https://en.wikipedia.org/wiki/Jerry_West

The Hoops Geek. (n.d.). The NBA Logo - History and Design. https://www.thehoopsgeek.com/nba-logo/

Yaron, Y. (2022, November 29). The history of the NBA logo: From Jerry West to Kobe Bryant. SB Nation. https://www.sbnation.com/nba/22300942/nba-logo-history-jerry-west-kobe-bryant

Fujita, S. (n.d.). Who Is on the NBA Logo? Scott Fujita. https://www.scottfujita.com/who-is-on-the-nba-logo/

LogoMyWay. (n.d.). History of the NBA Logo Design. https://blog.logomyway.com/history-nba-logo-design/

1000logos.net. (n.d.). NBA Logo - Design, History and Evolution. https://1000logos.net/nba-logo/

Andscape. (n.d.). Hall of Fame: The Designer of the NBA Logo. https://andscape.com/features/hall-of-fame-jerry-west-designer-alan-siegel-nba-logo/

Lines.com. (n.d.). Average Height of NBA Players - 2023. https://www.lines.com/guides/average-height-nba-players/1519

One37pm. (n.d.). The Tallest NBA Players of All Time. https://www.one37pm.com/sports/tallest-nba-players

Sportsnaut. (n.d.). The Shortest NBA Players in History. https://sportsnaut.com/shortest-nba-players/

Livestrong.com. (n.d.). Is Height Important in Basketball? https://www.livestrong.com/article/363066-is-height-important-in-basketball/

StatCrunch. (n.d.). Height and Points per Minute Played in the NBA. https://www.statcrunch.com/reports/view?reportid=16493&tab=preview

WritingBros. (n.d.). Correlation between the Height of NBA Players and the Average Points per Minute Played. https://writingbros.com/essay-examples/correlation-between-the-height-of-nba-players-and-the-average-points-per-minute-played/

HackaStat. (n.d.). Influence of Height in Basketball Performance. https://hackastat.eu/en/height-influence-in-basketball/

SLAM Online. (n.d.). Earl Boykins Is Shockingly Strong. https://www.slam-online.com/archives/earl-boykins-is-shockingly-strong/

Motivation and Love. (n.d.). Female Basketball Player Quotes. https://motivationandlove.com/female-basketball-player-quotes

WNBA. (n.d.). WNBA History. https://www.wnba.com/history/

Encyclopaedia Britannica. (n.d.). Women's National Basketball Association. https://www.britannica.com/topic/Womens-National-Basketball-Association

Women's National Basketball Association. (n.d.). Wikipedia. https://en.wikipedia.org/wiki/Women%27s_National_Basketball_Association

One37pm. (n.d.). The History of the WNBA: From Its Inception to Present Day. https://www.one37pm.com/sports/wnba-history

WNBA. (n.d.). 2023 WNBA Regular Season Tips Off Friday, May 19, Featuring Record-High 40 Games Per Team in League's 27th Season. https://www.wnba.com/news/2023-wnba-regular-season-tips-off-friday-may-19-featuring-record-high-40-games-per-team-in-leagues-27th-season

WNBA. (n.d.). Rules Changes for 2023 Season. https://www.wnba.com/news/rules-changes-for-2023-season

WNBA. (n.d.). WNBA Approves New Playoff Format. https://www.wnba.com/news/wnba-approves-new-playoff-format

Howard, J. (2023, May 19). International Players Are Making Their Mark on the WNBA Again. FiveThirtyEight. https://fivethirtyeight.com/features/international-players-are-making-their-mark-on-the-wnba-again/

Gracious Quotes. (n.d.). Sue Bird Quotes That Will Make You Want to Achieve More. https://graciousquotes.com/sue-bird/

Bleacher Report. (n.d.). Lauren Jackson, Sue Bird, and the 10 Greatest WNBA Players of All Time. https://bleacherreport.com/articles/583383-lauren-jackson-sue-bird-and-the-10-greatest-wnba-players-of-all-time

Wolfgang Sport. (n.d.). The 10 Best WNBA Players of All Time. https://www.wolfgangsport.com/best-wnba-players-of-all-time/

NBC Sports Chicago. (n.d.). Bird, Fowles Among Best WNBA Players of All Time. https://www.nbcsportschicago.com/wnba/bird-fowles-among-best-wnba-players-of-all-time/330142/

ESPN. (n.d.). WNBA's Greatest Players of All Time: Ranking the 25 Best in League History. https://www.espn.ph/wnba/story/_/id/32210623/wnba-greatest-players-all-ranking-25-best-league-history

AP News. (2023, July 21). Sue Bird to Have Seattle Storm Jersey Retired on Sept. 28. https://apnews.com/article/sue-bird-seattle-storm-jersey-retirement-e8747c78881b9363da04a6474d996d98

Nation World. (2022, July 27). Gold and Green: Olympic Basketball and NBA Business Intersect. Times Leader. https://www.timesleader.com/wire/nation-world/1505029/gold-and-green-olympic-basketball-nba-business-intersect

Olympic.org. (n.d.). Olympic Basketball History: The Dream Team, USA vs. Soviet Union. https://olympics.com/en/news/olympic-basketball-history-dream-team-usa-soviet-union

Basketball at the Summer Olympics. (n.d.). Wikipedia. https://en.wikipedia.org/wiki/Basketball_at_the_Summer_Olympics

Olympic.org. (n.d.). Basketball. https://stillmed.olympic.org/AssetsDocs/OSC%20Section/pdf/QR_sports_summer/Sports_olympiques%20_basketball%20_eng.pdf

Bleacher Report. (n.d.). The 10 Most Memorable Moments in Olympic Basketball History. https://bleacherreport.com/articles/1233921-the-10-most-memorable-moments-in-olympic-basketball-history

Sporting News. (n.d.). The Most Memorable Moments in Olympic Basketball History. https://www.sportingnews.com/au/nba/news/the-most-memorable-moments-in-olympic-basketball-history/7zzph63yocdd17jyu6y-4jqvb9

Sportskeeda. (n.d.). 5 Most Memorable Moments in Olympic Basketball.

https://www.sportskeeda.com/basketball/5-most-memorable-moments-olympic-basketball

Belz, A. (2018, August 16). How Basketball Became the World's Second-Biggest Sport. The Washington Post. https://www.washingtonpost.com/news/made-by-history/wp/2018/08/16/how-basketball-became-the-worlds-second-biggest-sport/

Bleacher Report. (n.d.). 7 Nations That Can Eventually Overtake USA Basketball Dominance. https://bleacherreport.com/articles/1272478-7-nations-that-can-eventually-overtake-usa-basketball-dominance

Badenhausen, K. (2016, August 17). The $255 Million Olympic Basketball Team. Forbes. https://www.forbes.com/sites/kurtbadenhausen/2016/08/17/the-255-million-olympic-basketball-team/?sh=164f44fa6609

History.com. (n.d.). Epic Sports Upsets: Olympics - United States vs. Soviet Union. https://www.history.com/news/epic-sports-upsets-olympics-united-states-soviet-union

ActiveSG Circle. (n.d.). What Is Wheelchair Basketball? https://www.activesgcircle.gov.sg/learn/basketball/what-is-wheelchair-basketball

Wheelchair Basketball. (n.d.). Wikipedia. https://en.wikipedia.org/wiki/Wheelchair_basketball

Wheelchair Basketball at the Summer Paralympics. (n.d.). Wikipedia. https://en.wikipedia.org/wiki/Wheelchair_basketball_at_the_Summer_Paralympics

Wheelchair Basketball. (n.d.). Paralympics Australia. https://www.paralympic.org.au/sports/wheelchair-basketball/

International Wheelchair Basketball Federation. (n.d.). The Game. https://iwbf.org/the-game/

United States Men's National Wheelchair Basketball Team. (n.d.). Wikipedia. https://en.wikipedia.org/wiki/United_States_men%27s_national_wheelchair_basketball_team

United States Women's National Wheelchair Basketball Team. (n.d.). Wikipedia. https://en.wikipedia.org/wiki/United_States_women%27s_national_wheelchair_basketball_team

National Wheelchair Basketball Association. (n.d.). https://www.nwba.org/usawb

International Paralympic Committee. (n.d.). USA's Men's Wheelchair Basketball Team Named. https://www.paralympic.org/news/usa-s-men-s-wheelchair-basketball-team-named

Sportskeeda. (n.d.). Team USA Paralympics Basketball: A Closer Look at Team Key Players. https://www.sportskeeda.com/basketball/team-usa-paralympics-basketball-a-closer-look-team-key-players

Goodreads. (n.d.). "I am America. I am the part you won't recognize." https://www.goodreads.com/quotes/74323-i-am-america-i-am-the-part-you-won-t-recognize

Library of Congress. (n.d.). Brown v. Board at Fifty: "With an Even Hand" | Brown v. Board of Education. https://www.loc.gov/exhibits/brown/brown-segregation.html

NBA. (n.d.). How Chuck Cooper, Nat Clifton, and Earl Lloyd Changed NBA Racial Integration. https://www.nba.com/news/how-chuck-cooper-nat-clifton-earl-lloyd-changed-nba-racial-integration

Naismith Memorial Basketball Hall of Fame. (n.d.). Charles "Chuck" Cooper. https://www.hoophall.com/hall-of-famers/charles-chuck-cooper/

BlackPast. (n.d.). The First Black Players in the NBA (1950). https://www.blackpast.org/african-american-history/the-first-black-players-in-the-nba-1950/

Sacramento Kings. (n.d.). Earl Lloyd: The Man Who Broke the NBA Color Barrier. https://www.nba.com/kings/blog/earl-lloyd-man-broke-nba-color-barrier

University of Virginia. (n.d.). The First Black Players in the NBA | Virtual Jamestown. https://xroads.virginia.edu/~CLASS/am483_97/projects/walters/Mjbball.html

Gettysburg College. (n.d.). Genetic Factors in Athletic Performance. https://cupola.gettysburg.edu/cgi/viewcontent.cgi?article=1767&context=stu-

dent_scholarship

Encyclopedia.com. (n.d.). Genetics and Athletic Performance. https://www.encyclopedia.com/social-sciences/encyclopedias-almanacs-transcripts-and-maps/genetics-and-athletic-performance

Sporting News. (n.d.). The Black Fives: A History of the Era That Led to the NBA's Racial Integration. https://www.sportingnews.com/ca/nba/news/the-black-fives-a-history-of-the-era-that-led-to-the-nbas-racial-integration/8fennuvt00hl1odmregcrbbtj

Wikipedia. (n.d.). Race and Ethnicity in the NBA. https://en.wikipedia.org/wiki/Race_and_ethnicity_in_the_NBA

The Root. (n.d.). Why Are There So Many Black Athletes? https://www.theroot.com/why-are-there-so-many-black-athletes-1790876918

Gale. (n.d.). The Achievements of Black American Athletes. https://blog.gale.com/the-achievements-of-black-american-athletes/

AARP. (n.d.). Barrier Breakers: A Tribute to Black Athletes. https://www.aarp.org/politics-society/history/info-2021/barrier-breakers-tribute-to-black-athletes.html

Hoopese. (n.d.). Why Are Most NBA Players Black? https://hoopese.com/why-are-most-nba-players-black/

NBA. (n.d.). Jersey Day: The Evolution of NBA Uniforms. https://www.nba.com/news/jersey-day-evolution-of-nba-uniform

Wikipedia. (n.d.). Basketball Uniform. https://en.wikipedia.org/wiki/Basketball_uniform

InterBasket. (n.d.). NBA Jerseys. https://www.interbasket.net/jerseys/nba/

This Is Basketball. (n.d.). A Comprehensive History of Basketball Uniforms. https://thisisbasketball.world/a-comprehensive-history-of-basketball-uniforms/?v=a25496ebf095

Just Love Basketball. (n.d.). Why Do NBA Players Wear Arm Sleeves? https://justlovebasketball.com/why-do-nba-players-wear-arm-sleeves/

Sportskeeda. (n.d.). Revisited: Michael Jordan, the Epitome of Show Biz |

Wilt Chamberlain Heaps High Praise on Michael Jordan, Says He's One of the Rare Specimens. https://www.sportskeeda.com/basketball/revisited-michael-epitome-show-biz-wilt-chamberlain-heaps-high-praise-michael-jordan-says-he-s-one-rare-specimens

Chicago Bulls. (n.d.). Michael Jordan. https://history.bulls.com/players/michael-jordan/

Bleacher Report. (n.d.). Michael Jordan: The Greatest of All Time. https://bleacherreport.com/articles/926592-michael-jordan-the-greatest-of-all-time

Fadeaway World. (n.d.). 10 Reasons Why Michael Jordan Is the GOAT. https://fadeawayworld.net/10-reasons-why-michael-jordan-is-the-goat

HowTheyPlay. (n.d.). Why Michael Jordan Is the GOAT (Greatest of All Time). https://howtheyplay.com/team-sports/Why-Michael-Jordan-is-the-GOAT-Greatest-of-All-Time

Wikipedia. (n.d.). Michael Jordan. https://en.wikipedia.org/wiki/Michael_Jordan

Republic World. (n.d.). Michael Jordan Inspired Generations of Athletes, Including LeBron & Woods. https://www.republicworld.com/sports-news/basketball-news/michael-jordan-inspired-generations-of-athletes-including-lebron-woods.html

Bleacher Report. (n.d.). Michael Jordan and His NBA Heirs: The 10 Most "Like Mike" Players in the League. https://bleacherreport.com/articles/537852-michael-jordan-and-his-nba-heirs-the-10-most-like-mike-players-in-the-league

Centuro Global. (n.d.). The Power of Partnerships: Nike & Michael Jordan. https://www.centuroglobal.com/article/the_power_of_partnerships_nike_michael_jordan

The Guardian. (n.d.). Michael Jordan Changed the World: The True Story Behind Nike Movie "Air." https://www.theguardian.com/film/2023/apr/05/michael-jordan-changed-the-world-the-true-story-behind-nike-movie-air

Sporting News. (n.d.). Michael Jordan's Flu Game: Bulls in NBA Finals. https://www.sportingnews.com/us/nba/news/michael-jordan-flu-game-bulls-nba-finals/j5zgcbpulmj2wcislyynphsr

Facts.net. (n.d.). 55 Facts about Michael Jordan. https://facts.net/michael-jordan-facts/

USA Today. (n.d.). 60 Fun Facts about Michael Jordan on His 60th Birthday. https://www.usatoday.com/story/sports/nba/2023/02/16/michael-jordan-60th-birthday-60-fun-facts-basketball-legend/11264902002/

People. (n.d.). Kareem Abdul-Jabbar Honors Kobe Bryant on 8/24 with Praise for Seemingly "Bad" Game Statistic. https://people.com/sports/kareem-abdul-jabbar-honors-kobe-bryant-8-24-with-praise-for-seemingly-bad-game-statistic/

The Athletic. (n.d.). Forgotten Fridays: How Kobe Bryant Became the Youngest Player to Start an NBA Game 25 Years Ago. https://theathletic.com/3094234/2022/01/28/forgotten-fridays-how-kobe-bryant-became-the-youngest-player-to-start-an-nba-game-25-years-ago/

Yardbarker. (n.d.). Kobe Bryant's 40 Greatest Moments. https://www.yardbarker.com/nba/articles/kobe_bryants_40_greatest_moments/s1__27075788#slide_1

NBA. (n.d.). Kobe Bryant Tribute. https://www.nba.com/kobe-bryant-tribute

ReadWrite. (n.d.). The Amazing Success Story of Basketball Player Kobe Bryant. https://readwrite.com/the-amazing-success-story-of-basketball-player-kobe-bryant/

Britannica. (n.d.). Kobe Bryant. https://www.britannica.com/biography/Kobe-Bryant

Stacker. (n.d.). Kobe Bryant: A Life Story You May Not Know. https://stacker.com/celebrities/kobe-bryant-life-story-you-may-not-know

Marca. (n.d.). Kobe Bryant, the Eternal Laker, Would Have Turned 44 Today. https://www.marca.com/en/basketball/nba/los-angeles-lakers/2023/01/26/63d29b58ca4741ff128b45b2.html

Bleacher Report. (n.d.). Michael Jordan Says "When Kobe Bryant Died, a Piece of Me Died." https://bleacherreport.com/articles/2877803-michael-jordan-says-when-kobe-bryant-died-a-piece-of-me-died

T-Bones Baseball. (n.d.). Why Professional Athletes Go Bankrupt. https://tbonesbaseball.com/why-professional-athletes-go-bankrupt/

Essentially Sports. (n.d.). Despite 65 Percent of NBA Players Going Broke within 5 Years of Retirement, Shaquille O'Neal's Mother Helped Him Buy 175 Restaurants and Amass $450 Million Net Worth. https://www.essentially-sports.com/nba-basketball-news-despite-65-percent-of-nba-players-going-broke-within-5-years-of-retirement-shaquille-oneals-mother-helped-him-buy-175-restaurants-and-amass-450-million-net-worth/

Investopedia. (n.d.). Why Athletes Go Broke. https://www.investopedia.com/financial-edge/0312/why-athletes-go-broke.aspx

Yahoo Sports. (n.d.). 15 Athletes Who Went Broke After Retirement. https://sports.yahoo.com/ys-investopediamoneyloss031010.html

Reddit. (n.d.). 60% of NBA Players Broke 5 Years After Retirement. https://www.reddit.com/r/sports/comments/cm666/60_of_nba_players_broke_5_years_after_retirement/

Wikipedia. (n.d.). Personal Finances of Professional American Athletes. https://en.wikipedia.org/wiki/Personal_finances_of_professional_American_athletes

Fadeaway World. (n.d.). 20 NBA Players Who Went Broke and Lost Millions of Dollars. https://fadeawayworld.net/nba/20-nba-players-who-went-broke-and-lost-millions-of-dollars

Cyndeowp. (n.d.). The Five Main Reasons Professional Athletes Go Broke. [Website]. Retrieved from https://cyndeowp.com/the-five-main-reasons-professional-athletes-go-broke/

University of Washington School of Medicine. (n.d.). NCAA Basketball Players More Prone to Sudden Cardiac Death. [News Article]. Retrieved from https://newsroom.uw.edu/story/ncaa-basketball-players-more-prone-sudden-cardiac-death

University of Rochester Medical Center. (n.d.). Basketball Injuries. [Webpage]. Retrieved from https://www.urmc.rochester.edu/orthopaedics/sports-medicine/basketball-injuries.shtml

Bleacher Report. (n.d.). Marquis Daniels and the Most Horrific On-Court NBA Injuries Ever. [Webpage]. Retrieved from https://bleacherreport.com/articles/600493-marquis-daniels-and-the-most-horrific-on-court-nba-injuries-ever

Sports Brief. (n.d.). NBA Players Who Died on the Court: Ballers Passed Doing What They Loved. [Webpage]. Retrieved from https://sportsbrief.com/nba/25041-nba-players-died-court-ballers-passed-what-love/

UAB Medicine. (n.d.). Basketball Players Suffer the Highest Rate of Sudden Cardiac Death. [Webpage]. Retrieved from https://www.uabmedicine.org/news/basketball-players-suffer-the-highest-rate-of-sudden-cardiac-death/

The Kansas City Star. (n.d.). [Article Title Not Available]. [News Article]. Retrieved from https://www.kansascity.com/news/nation-world/national/article272063947.html

ESPN. (n.d.). The Tragedy of Hank Gathers, the Triumph of Loyola Marymount. [News Article]. Retrieved from https://www.espn.com/mens-college-basketball/story/_/id/30880702/the-tragedy-hank-gathers-triumph-loyola-marymount

ESPN. (n.d.). Remembering Reggie Lewis: 20 Years After Tragic Death. [News Article]. Retrieved from https://www.espn.com/boston/nba/story/_/id/9510589/remembering-reggie-lewis-20-years-tragic-death

The Guardian. (2023, February 17). Slam Dunk Banned in College Basketball and High School. [News Article]. Retrieved from https://www.theguardian.com/sport/2023/feb/17/slam-dunk-banned-college-basketball-high-school

Wikipedia. (n.d.). Slam Dunk. [Webpage]. Retrieved from https://en.wikipedia.org/wiki/Slam_dunk

Red Bull. (n.d.). Slam Dunk: The History of the Slam Dunk. [Webpage].

Retrieved from https://www.redbull.com/us-en/slam-dunk-history

Sportskeeda. (n.d.). The History of the Slam Dunk Shot in Basketball. [Webpage]. Retrieved from https://www.sportskeeda.com/basketball/history-slam-dunk-shot-basketball

Interbasket. (n.d.). Who Invented the Slam Dunk? History Behind the Dunk. [Webpage]. Retrieved from https://www.interbasket.net/news/who-invented-the-slam-dunk-history-behind-the-dunk/7722/

Franchise Sports. (n.d.). The Greatest Dunks of All Time. [Webpage]. Retrieved from https://franchisesports.co.uk/greatest-dunks-of-all-time/

The Sporting Blog. (n.d.). Best Dunkers in NBA History. [Webpage]. Retrieved from https://thesporting.blog/blog/best-dunkers-in-nba-history

Wikipedia. (n.d.). Vince Carter. [Webpage]. Retrieved from https://en.wikipedia.org/wiki/Vince_Carter

Basketball Reference. (n.d.). Vince Carter. [Webpage]. Retrieved from https://www.basketball-reference.com/players/c/cartevi01.html

Cypher Sessions. (n.d.). Air Canada Lands for the Last Time: Vince Carter Officially Retires After 22 NBA Seasons. [Webpage]. Retrieved from https://cyphersessions.co/2020/06/25/air-canada-lands-for-the-last-time-vince-carter-officially-retires-after-22-nba-seasons/

Bleacher Report. (n.d.). Defying Gravity: Vince Carter's Top 10 Dunks. [Webpage]. Retrieved from https://bleacherreport.com/articles/450405-defying-gravity-vince-carters-top-10-dunks

Fox Sports. (n.d.). Vince Carter Describes Greatest NBA Dunk Contest That Never Happened. [Webpage]. Retrieved from https://www.foxsports.com/stories/nba/vince-carter-describes-greatest-nba-dunk-contest-that-never-happened

The Athletic. (n.d.). For Vince Carter, Dunking Was Like Ordering Fast Food: What Are My Options? [News Article]. Retrieved from https://theathletic.com/2502956/2021/04/09/for-vince-carter-dunking-was-like-ordering-fast-food-what-are-my-options/

Wikipedia. (n.d.). Harlem Globetrotters. [Webpage]. Retrieved from https://

en.wikipedia.org/wiki/Harlem_Globetrotters

Encyclopedia Britannica. (n.d.). Harlem Globetrotters. [Webpage]. Retrieved from https://www.britannica.com/topic/Harlem-Globetrotters

Harlem Globetrotters. (n.d.). About. [Webpage]. Retrieved from https://www.harlemglobetrotters.com/about/

Quora. (n.d.). What Are the Harlem Globetrotters? [Webpage]. Retrieved from https://www.quora.com/What-are-the-Harlem-Globetrotters

WTTW Interactive. (n.d.). Harlem Globetrotters. [Webpage]. Retrieved from https://interactive.wttw.com/dusable-to-obama/harlem-globetrotters

History.com. (n.d.). 10 Things You May Not Know About the Harlem Globetrotters. [Webpage]. Retrieved from https://www.history.com/news/10-things-you-may-not-know-about-the-harlem-globetrotters

Scout Life. (n.d.). Cool Facts About the Harlem Globetrotters. [Webpage]. Retrieved from https://headsup.scoutlife.org/cool-facts-harlem-globetrotters/

Neatorama. (n.d.). 17 Facts About The Harlem Globetrotters. [Webpage]. Retrieved from https://www.neatorama.com/2014/08/22/17-Facts-About-The-Harlem-Globetrotters/

Minimalist Quotes. (n.d.). LeBron James Quote. [Webpage]. Retrieved from https://minimalistquotes.com/lebron-james-quote-10497/

Notable Biographies. (n.d.). LeBron James. [Webpage]. Retrieved from https://www.notablebiographies.com/news/Ge-La/James-LeBron.html

Wikipedia. (n.d.). LeBron James. [Webpage]. Retrieved from https://en.wikipedia.org/wiki/LeBron_James

Fadeaway World. (n.d.). NBA Fan Shares LeBron James' Inspiring Life Story and How He Stayed Humble. [Webpage]. Retrieved from https://fadeawayworld.net/nba-media/nba-fan-shares-lebron-james-inspiring-life-story-and-how-he-stayed-humble-with-the-perfect-reputation-no-education-no-father-no-training-and-few-role-models

Bleacher Report. (n.d.). Jeremy Lin and the Most Improbable Success Stories in Sports. [Webpage]. Retrieved from https://bleacherreport.com/articles/1062765-jeremy-lin-and-the-most-improbable-success-stories-in-sports

The Nation. (n.d.). Jeremy Lin Inspires a Nation. [News Article]. Retrieved from https://www.thenation.com/article/archive/jeremy-lin-inspires-nation/

Basketball University. (n.d.). Jeremy Lin: The NBA's Great Tragedy. [Webpage]. Retrieved from https://medium.com/basketball-university/jeremy-lin-the-nbas-great-tragedy-97880aa1f446

Basha Bears Basketball. (n.d.). The Rise of Kevin Durant: From Humble Beginnings to NBA Stardom. [Webpage]. Retrieved from https://bashabears-basketball.com/the-rise-of-kevin-durant-from-humble-beginnings-to-nba-stardom/

Encyclopedia Britannica. (n.d.). Kevin Durant. [Webpage]. Retrieved from https://www.britannica.com/biography/Kevin-Durant

Wikipedia. (n.d.). Kevin Durant. [Webpage]. Retrieved from https://en.wikipedia.org/wiki/Kevin_Durant

Ducksters. (n.d.). Kevin Durant. [Webpage]. Retrieved from https://www.ducksters.com/sports/kevin_durant.php

Bleacher Report. (n.d.). NBA Trades: The Best Trade Made in the History of Every Team. [Webpage]. Retrieved from https://bleacherreport.com/articles/771942-nba-trades-the-best-trade-made-in-the-history-of-every-team

Bleacher Report. (n.d.). 10 Biggest Blockbuster Trades in NBA History. [Webpage]. Retrieved from https://bleacherreport.com/articles/1250593-10-biggest-blockbuster-trades-in-nba-history

Wikipedia. (n.d.). Sign-and-Trade Deal. [Webpage]. Retrieved from https://en.wikipedia.org/wiki/Sign-and-trade_deal

Hoops Addict. (n.d.). NBA Trade Rules Explained. [Webpage]. Retrieved from https://www.hoopsaddict.com/nba-trade-rules-explained/

Field Insider. (n.d.). All You Need to Know About NBA Trade Rules. [Webpage]. Retrieved from https://fieldinsider.com/all-you-need-to-know-about-nba-trade-rules/

Hoopshype. (n.d.). This Is How Trades Go Down in the NBA. [Webpage]. Retrieved from https://hoopshype.com/2017/02/21/this-is-how-trades-go-down-in-the-nba/

Fox Sports. (n.d.). Why NBA Trades Have Grown More Complicated. [Webpage]. Retrieved from https://www.foxsports.com/stories/nba/why-nba-trades-have-grown-more-complicated

ESPN. (n.d.). Ranking Some of the Biggest Trades in Two Decades: How They Inform Kevin Durant's Future. [Webpage]. Retrieved from https://www.espn.com/nba/story/_/id/34277696/ranking-some-biggest-trades-two-decades-how-inform-kevin-durant-future

The Sportster. (n.d.). Top 10 NBA Players with Weird Superstitions. [Webpage]. Retrieved from https://www.thesportster.com/basketball/top-10-nba-players-with-weird-superstitions/#4-rajon-rondo

Bleacher Report. (n.d.). 7 Strange NBA Superstitions You Have to Read to Believe. [Webpage]. Retrieved from https://bleacherreport.com/articles/1120943-7-strange-nba-superstitions-you-have-to-read-to-believ

Basketball Network. (n.d.). The 5 Strangest NBA Superstitions Players Couldn't Function Without. [Webpage]. Retrieved from https://www.basketballnetwork.net/off-the-court/the-5-strangest-nba-superstitions-players-couldnt-function-without

Ranker. (n.d.). The Best NBA Superstitions. [Webpage]. Retrieved from https://www.ranker.com/list/best-nba-superstitions/patrick-alexander

McDavid USA. (n.d.). Insane Professional Basketball Pre-Game Rituals You Won't Believe. [Webpage]. Retrieved from https://www.mcdavidusa.com/blogs/posts/insane-professional-basketball-pre-game-rituals-wont-believe

Sports Illustrated. (n.d.). Basketball Superstitions Throughout History. [Webpage]. Retrieved from https://www.si.com/nba/cavaliers/nba/cavaliers/nba-amico/basketball-superstitions-throughout-history

Basketball Insiders. (n.d.). NBA AM: NBA Player Superstitions. [Webpage]. Retrieved from https://www.basketballinsiders.com/news/nba-am-nba-player-superstitions/

CBS Sports. (n.d.). Here's Why LeBron James Got Rid of the Headband This Season. [Webpage]. Retrieved from https://www.cbssports.com/nba/news/heres-why-lebron-james-got-rid-of-the-headband-this-season/

www.ingramcontent.com/pod-product-compliance
Lightning Source LLC
Chambersburg PA
CBHW071203070526
44584CB00019B/2901